D&S
VOL. 36

THE WORLD'S
FIRST SUPER CARRIER

ALSO INCLUDES COVERAGE OF
CARRIER AIR WING SIX!

USS FORRESTAL

A DETAIL & SCALE AVIATION PUBLICATION

in detail & scale

D1605029

Bert Kinzey

TAB BOOKS
Blue Ridge Summit, PA

Airlife Publishing Ltd.
England

This book is a product of Detail & Scale, Inc., which has sole responsibility for its content and layout, except that all contributors are responsible for the security clearance and copyright release of all materials submitted. Published and distributed in the United States by TAB BOOKS, and in Great Britain and Europe by Airlife Publishing Ltd.

CONTRIBUTORS AND SOURCES:

Donnie Head
USS FORRESTAL
COMNAVAIRLANT Public Affairs Office
U. S. Navy
National Archives
Department of Defense Still Media Records Center

A special acknowledgment is due to LCDR Mike John and LT Paul Jenkins at the public affairs office of COMNAVAIRLANT. The author is most grateful for their assistance, cooperation, and support.

A very special word of thanks is expressed to LT Marv Mashke, the public affairs officer aboard FORRESTAL, for his help, patience, and kindness.

Many photographs in this book are credited to their contributors. Photographs with no credit indicated were taken by the author.

FIRST EDITION
FIRST PRINTING

Published in United States by

TAB BOOKS
Blue Ridge Summit, PA 17294-0214

Library of Congress Cataloging
in Publication Data:

Kinzey, Bert.
USS Forrestal / by Bert Kinzey.
p.   cm. — (Detail & scale ; v. 36)
ISBN 0-8306-7049-1
1. Forrestal (Aircraft carrier) I. Title.
VA65.F66K56   1990
359.3′255—dc   90-35163
                                CIP

First published in Great Britain in 1990
by Airlife Publishing Ltd.
7 St. John's Hill, Shrewsbury, SY1 1JE

British Library Cataloging in
Publication Data
Kinzey, Bert, 1945-
USS Forrestal.
1. United States. Navy. Aircraft carriers
I. Title II. Detail and scale series
623.82550974

ISBN 1-85310-621-6

TAB BOOKS offers software for
sale. For information and a catalog,
please contact TAB Software Department,
Blue Ridge Summit, PA 17294-0850.

Questions regarding the content of this book
should be addressed to:

Reader Inquiry Branch
TAB BOOKS
Blue Ridge Summit, PA 17294-0214

Front cover: This photograph, taken from almost directly overhead, provides an excellent look at the details of FORRESTAL's huge flight deck. The layout of the four catapults and four elevators is clearly visible. The photograph was taken by the author in July 1989.

Rear cover: This dramatic view shows many of FORRESTAL's details. Around the ship are placed the insignias of Carrier Air Wing Six and its squadrons.

INTRODUCTION

FORRESTAL is shown here shortly after she began operational service. The jet fighters on the forward catapults are McDonnell Banshees, as are those parked back near the superstructure. Swept-winged, North American Furies are spotted to port on the angled deck, and propeller-driven Douglas Skyraiders are positioned further aft.

(National Archives)

This is the third volume in the Detail & Scale Series written about one of the U.S. Navy's aircraft carriers. Volume 29 covered the USS LEXINGTON, while volume 34 was on the USS AMERICA. This new title is about the USS FORRESTAL, a ship which is historically significant because she was the world's first super carrier. FORRESTAL was the first aircraft carrier designed and built after World War II, the first built with a canted or angled deck, and the first designed to operate jet aircraft. Her design was a considerable step forward over the previous MIDWAY and ESSEX classes, and this design has proved so successful that it has remained the basis for all U.S. carriers that have been constructed since FORRESTAL was launched on December 11, 1954.

Since LEXINGTON has the most extensive history of any American aircraft carrier, our narrative in that book was concerned primarily with the ship's operational history that included all of the major battles in the Pacific during World War II. It also covered the ESSEX class modernizations in considerable detail. In our book on AMERICA, Detail & Scale provided a look at the rigorous operational schedules followed by the U.S. Navy's carriers and their crews. These schedules include yard periods for maintenance and modernizations, periods of training, evaluations, qualifications, and extended cruises all over the globe. Since FORRESTAL was the first super carrier, and because her design represented such significant changes and improvements over previous classes, it is fitting that the narrative of this book should provide some insight into the factors that determined her final design.

As with our other two titles on aircraft carriers, almost one-half of the book is taken up with scores of photographs that show the major details of the ship. Everything from the anchors to the rudders and the radars to the engine rooms are covered with detailed photographs, almost all of which were taken specifically for this publication. The catapults, arresting gear, fresnel lens, radar antenna, weapons systems, bridges, hangar deck, elevators, and much more are shown in extensive detail. A look at Carrier Air Wing Six is also provided. It includes all of the types of aircraft presently embarked in FORRESTAL and illustrates their markings. Rounding out this book is our usual modeler's section which covers the scale model kits available of the FORRESTAL. This should be of particular interest to scale modelers because of the recent releases of the 1/720th scale FORRESTAL by Italeri/Testors, and the reworked Revell FORRESTAL kit.

SHIP'S HISTORY

This artist's concept shows one of several designs considered for the USS UNITED STATES, CVB-58. This flush-decked ship would have been the first super carrier had it not been cancelled shortly after construction began.
(National Archives)

Throughout most of the history of fighting ships, the prides of the major navies of the world have been the biggest ships with the biggest guns. In the days of sail, ships like the USS CONSTITUTION, nicknamed "Old Ironsides," typified the efforts to build stronger ships with more and more guns. These ships would move up next to an adversary and slug it out until a victor was decided. This "big ship, big gun" thinking continued well into the twentieth century, long after the wooden ships had given way to those made of steel, and sails had been replaced by propellers turned by mighty steam-driven engines. The dreadnoughts became the ships that ruled the seas, and the world's major naval powers continued to seek ways to put more firepower and armored protection in their battleships.

But the invention of the airplane was destined to change everything, although this change took many years due to the stubbornness and shortsightedness of the "battleship admirals" that controlled the U. S. Navy during the first four decades of the twentieth century. The demise of the battleship as the principle naval combatant began on November 14, 1910, when Eugene Ely made the first flight from the deck of a ship at Hampton Roads, Virginia. Ely took off from an 83-foot long sloping deck that had been constructed on the cruiser USS BIRMINGHAM. On January 18, 1911, Ely accomplished the more difficult task of making the first landing aboard a ship when he set his Curtiss pusher down a 120-foot long deck that had been built on the battleship USS PENNSYLVANIA. Within an hour after he landed, Ely turned the aircraft around and successfully took off from the PENNSYLVANIA. Naval shipboard aviation was born, and although it would be another thirty years before the true impact of naval aviation was realized, Ely's accomplishments, along with those of other pioneers like Glenn

Curtiss, were destined to change the focus of naval power forever.

For many years there were "experts" that continued to believe that the battleship would remain the primary capital ship. They argued that the armor carried by these awesome ships would protect them from any bomb an aircraft might carry, and their gun batteries would shoot down the aircraft before it got close enough to attack the battleship. But Billy Mitchell showed the folly of this thinking on July 21, 1921. After unsuccessful attempts with smaller bombs, he and his pilots sank the captured German battleship OSTFRIESLAND with 2000-pound bombs.

Although there were many people who still believed that the battleship would always remain the ruler of the seas, more and more emphasis was placed on aviation in all branches of the service. The U. S. Navy developed land-based, sea-based, and carrier-based aircraft in the years between World War I and World War II. Aircraft carriers, beginning with the converted collier LANGLEY (CV-1), were added to the fleet. Built on the hulls of battlecruisers, LEXINGTON (CV-2) and SARATOGA (CV-3) followed LANGLEY, and RANGER (CV-4) became the first U. S. aircraft carrier designed and built as such from the keel up. WASP (CV-7) and the three ships of the YORKTOWN class rounded out the pre-war carrier construction for the U. S. Navy. In addition to YORKTOWN (CV-5), ENTERPRISE (CV-6) and HORNET (CV-8) comprised this last pre-war class.

By the end of 1941, the Japanese had erased any lingering doubts about the capabilities of carrier-based aircraft, and the battleship had been relegated to a supporting role. Throughout World War II, very few surface battles were fought between major combatants, which was the type of warfare the battleship was designed for.

Instead, battleships provided anti-aircraft fire to protect the fleet, and used their big guns for off-shore bombardment of land-based targets.

Also by the end of 1941, the first ships of the new ESSEX class of fleet carriers were being built, and ESSEX (CV-9) herself was commissioned at the end of the following year. Thirteen ships in this class would serve in the Pacific in World War II, and along with the light carriers of the INDEPENDENCE class, would establish themselves as the principle warships in the U. S. Navy. Numerous smaller escort carriers would also join the war effort, and most of these operated in the Atlantic protecting convoys.

American aircraft carriers roamed the Pacific throughout the war, and from mid-1943, spearheaded the attacks that moved closer and closer to the Japanese homeland. Within two years, carrier based aircraft were bombing Japan itself. It seemed that the aircraft carrier was destined to be the major instrument of naval power for as far into the future as anyone could see.

But at the end of World War II everything had changed. Two technological advances had cast dark shadows over the future of the aircraft carrier, and it appeared that these ships that had so recently ruled the seas might become obsolete. One of these advances was the jet engine which was destined to replace the reciprocating engine in military aircraft. Jets posed many considerable problems for carrier operations. Their flying characteristics caused several of these problems. Stronger catapults could be developed to make up for the fact that heavier jets with their slower acceleration could not simply "run the deck" as propeller-driven aircraft had done throughout much of the war. Catapults had been used during World War II, and their use had become more and more common toward the end of the war. But their use would be a requirement, not an option, with jet aircraft. Jets were very poor when it came to flying on the back side of the power curve. While they were certainly faster than their propeller-driven predecessors, they were not very good at flying slowly just above stall speed. This was an important characteristic for any aircraft that was going to land aboard a ship. Arresting gear could be developed that was strong enough to stop jet aircraft, but jets also had to be designed that could fly slow enough to land on a carrier and engage this arresting gear. This was not too difficult with the early jets with straight wings, but as the designs for jet aircraft progressed, the compatibility between the aircraft and the existing carriers grew further and further apart.

Jets also used more fuel than piston-driven engines, and space had to be found to store this fuel on the carriers. Deck handling of the huge blowtorches posed even more problems. Fortunately, the aircraft designers solved many of the problems. In the early 1950s it looked like land-based aircraft flown by the U. S. Air Force were going to far outperform anything that could operate from a ship, but by the end of the decade, the Navy's F8U Crusader was on a par with any of the fighters in the Air Force. By the mid-1960s, the Air Force found itself ordering the Navy's F-4 Phantom, and later the A-7 Corsair. Both of these were originally designed as carrier based jet aircraft. But changes to the jets could not solve all of the problems. Carrier design had to be advanced as well, and this was the other half of the equation as we shall see later.

The second advance that looked like it might spell the end of the carrier was the development of the atomic bomb. At the end of World War II, this awesome new weapon had dramatically altered the concept of war. The "experts" began to argue that almost every previous weapon, tactic, and concept was now obsolete. Tanks, ships, and foot soldiers would never be used in a war again, since they would easily be eliminated in mass with atomic weapons. In the United States, military planners spent almost all of their time and efforts on two concerns. One was to develop a nuclear delivery capability that would be so potentially destructive that no nation would dare attack America for fear of a retaliation that would be far greater than it could survive. The second concern was to develop a defense against the nuclear delivery systems of foreign nations, specifically the Soviet Union, so that no nuclear attack against the United States would be successful. Beyond these two primary concerns, everything else was of relatively little importance. Conventional forces of all kinds were scrapped or taken out of service and stored. In the post-war years, budget constraints compounded the problem. Strategic offensive and defensive systems got almost all of the funds that were available.

Early atomic bombs were so large and heavy that no carrier-based aircraft in existence or even designed at the end of the war could carry one. The Navy's plans to develop a nuclear bomber that could operate from carriers were expected to produce an aircraft weighing 100,000 pounds, far heavier than any aircraft that had ever flown from or landed on a ship. This bomber would not be able to operate from any existing carrier, so a new super carrier had to be built. There was a considerable amount of argument among the planners. Some were in favor of a carrier designed specifically to operate these nuclear bombers. This program, designated CVB-X, proposed a ship that would not even have a hangar, since the bombers would be far too large to fit into one. Other planners opted for a multi-purpose carrier which would embark an air group of both these nuclear bombers and smaller escorting fighters and other tactical aircraft. Such a carrier would have a hangar for the smaller aircraft. Regardless of which one of these carriers would be built, it would have to be a flush deck design, because the large wingspan of the bombers would make flight operations unsafe if a conventional island structure rose above the flight deck level. This would be particularly true during landing operations as the huge aircraft recovered on the ship's axial flight deck.

The fight for a new carrier was not simply a battle over a ship. It was an attempt by the Navy to gain a share of the nation's nuclear strike capability. Considering the importance of this capability when it came to priorities in planning and funding, the Navy's desire to be included in America's nuclear strike forces can be readily understood. It was feared that if the Navy did not have a share of this capability, it would become a "second rate" service in funding considerations and in any future war. After dominating the sea battles during World War II, it looked as though the carrier might now lose the battle for its very existence because of a weapon developed initially in the United States. Thus it seemed imperative for the Navy to come up with a carrier that could operate aircraft which could deliver the atomic bomb.

The first of these super carriers was finally authorized in July 1948 under the FY 1949 budget. It was designed to be a multi-purpose carrier embarking both the strategic bombers and other aircraft in its air wing. It would be able to operate jet aircraft far more efficiently than previous carriers, and had two small retractable islands. Also included in its design were four catapults, two forward, and one on each side on flight deck overhangs. There were also four elevators, one of which was located on the aft end of the flight deck. Defensive armament was comprised of five-inch/54 and three-inch/70 guns. It had an open bow, and the smoke stacks were mounted horizontally at the edges of the flight deck. It would be 1089 feet long, and its flight deck was 190 feet wide. Beam at the waterline was 130 feet. Its standard displacement was estimated to be 65,000 tons, and it would displace 80,000 tons at full load. Cost was estimated to be between 124 and 189 million dollars. Named the USS UNITED STATES, and designated CVB-58, the keel of this ship was laid on April 18, 1949, with the approval of both the President and Congress.

Only five days later, on April 23, 1949, Secretary of Defense Louis Johnson, without consulting the President, the Congress, or even the Chief of Naval Operations, cancelled the carrier. He did so at the urging of the newly established U. S. Air Force, and to a lesser degree, the U. S. Army. Both of these services wanted to strip the Navy of its nuclear capability in an effort to get more

The keel was laid for the USS UNITED STATES, but budget constraints caused its cancellation only a few days later.   *(National Archives)*

funding for themselves. At the same time, the Army was trying to have the Marines eliminated, thus further reducing the scope and funding for the Navy and gaining all funding for land-based, ground-gaining forces for itself. The Air Force wanted funds for the B-36, which it claimed was the best option for the delivery of nuclear weapons. It further made the absurd claim that the B-36 was invulnerable! It has been reported that a Navy pilot volunteered to intercept a B-36 and shoot it down to illustrate how ridiculous such a claim was. The Air Force appeared interested only in preparing for nuclear war, but the Navy's position was that the nation had to prepare for both nuclear and conventional warfare. The argument as to how much military spending should be for strategic forces versus conventional forces still continues today.

The loss of the USS UNITED STATES did not cause the Navy to give up the fight. It continued with the development of an aircraft that could deliver nuclear weapons from the three existing MIDWAY class carriers. This aircraft took the form of the North American AJ Savage, and the Navy attained a very limited shipboard nuclear delivery capability with the Savage in late 1950. Although it had temporarily lost the battle for a super carrier, the Navy had at least maintained a small portion of America's nuclear strike capability.

Even after the UNITED STATES was cancelled, the Navy did not give up the idea of building super carriers. Georgia's Carl Vinson predicted that Congress would eventually approve funding for another ship, but it was the North Koreans that cast the deciding vote. When the hostilities in Korea started in 1950, it proved that the United States needed to be fully prepared for a conventional war as well as a nuclear one. With the communists almost pushing the South Koreans and Americans off of the peninsula, eliminating air bases on land in the process, the need for more and better aircraft carriers became evident. It was Secretary of Defense Johnson, the man who had cancelled the USS UNITED STATES, that had to authorize new carrier construction. USS FORRESTAL was ordered on July 1951, and was included in the FY 1952 budget.

In the meantime, more technological advances had been made in the designs of jet aircraft and nuclear weapons. As stated earlier, aeronautical engineers were fast learning how to design high performance jets that could fly on to and off of carriers. But there were equally dramatic changes in the development of nuclear weapons. Most importantly, the size and weight of the weapons were being reduced considerably. It was not long before nuclear bombs were small enough and light enough for even the diminutive and forthcoming A4D Skyhawk to carry. This meant that even the older and smaller carriers, once converted and modernized, could operate aircraft that could deliver nuclear weapons. The large carrier-based bomber had shrunk in size from the previous 100,000 pounds to 70,000 pounds, and was being developed in the form of the A3D Skywarrior.

Today, all of the Navy's carriers are nuclear capable,

Taken from the bow and looking aft, this photograph shows FORRESTAL under construction at the Newport News Shipbuilding and Drydock Company.

(National Archives)

Troughs for catapults one and two are visible in the forward end of the flight deck as work continues on FORRESTAL's construction.　(National Archives)

but when nuclear weapons are aboard, they are tactical, not strategic weapons. The strategic nuclear capability of the Navy is considerable, and is at sea in submarines that carry ballistic missiles. It is doubtful that aircraft carriers will again become part of this nation's strategic forces in the future, but in the intervening years, the carrier has more than proved its worth as a vital part of America's defense capability. After playing an important role during the Korean War, they were constantly on Yankee and Dixie Stations in the Gulf of Tonkin pounding the enemy during the war in Vietnam. Fortunately, there have been no nuclear wars, but conventional wars have been waged constantly somewhere on this planet. Sometimes they involve the interests and the security of the United States. When such a "hot spot" flares up almost anywhere on the globe, it is one or more of these carriers that is sent to make a show of force and determination, and if necessary, participate in putting out the fire.

FORRESTAL was originally designated CVB-59, with the letters CVB being the Navy's designator for a large aircraft carrier. But this designation was later changed to CVA-59 on October 1, 1952, to reflect the ship's mission as an attack aircraft carrier rather than its size. She remained CVA-59 until being redesignated CV-59 on June 30, 1975, indicating the change to the CV Concept that became necessary with the retirement of the Navy's ASW support carriers and the development of more sophisticated and capable anti-submarine aircraft. As the

first super carrier to be built, she was named for former Secretary of the Navy James Vincent Forrestal, who had become the first Secretary of Defense in 1947. FORRESTAL thus became the first aircraft carrier designed and built after World War II.

Although aircraft designs were becoming more suitable for carrier operations, not all of the changes necessary to permit jet aircraft to effectively operate from ships could be made to the aircraft themselves. Some improvements and modifications had to be made to the designs of the ships, and FORRESTAL's design included these considerations. FORRESTAL was the first carrier designed specifically to operate jet aircraft. It was also the first to be designed with an enclosed bow since the first LEXINGTON and SARATOGA were built on battlecruiser hulls.

But even when her keel was laid on July 14, 1952, FORRESTAL's design had not been fully determined. It was originally intended that she have an axial landing deck and four catapults and four elevators laid out in much the same way as on the aborted USS UNITED STATES. At one time consideration was given to reducing the number of catapults and elevators to three each as a weight saving measure. As with the UNITED STATES, a retractable island was also included in the design. In fact, the statistics for FORRESTAL were very similar to those that had been proposed for the cancelled UNITED STATES. FORRESTAL's standard displacement was to be 59,000 tons, while a full load would displace just over 79,000 tons. Overall length was to be 1039 feet, the beam was 129.5 feet at the waterline, and the draft was 36 feet. FORRESTAL machinery included eight Babcock and Wilcox boilers and four Westinghouse geared turbine engines. With 260,000 shaft horsepower driving four five-bladed propellers, each twenty-one feet in diameter, the top speed would be thirty-three knots. By the time she was built, the three-inch gun was considered ineffective against modern aircraft, so FORRESTAL's original defensive armament consisted of only eight five-inch/54, Mk 42 guns. These were in single mounts, and were located in pairs on the bows and quarters of the ship. The cost to build FORRESTAL came to $188.9 million.

The British were also working hard at improving carrier designs, and it was one of their ideas that had the most dramatic effect on FORRESTAL's design and the design of all future carriers. The British had come up with the concept of landing aircraft at an angle to the ship's centerline rather that straight down the axial deck. Early experiments had shown that this concept was practical, and the U. S. Navy built a quickly installed angle deck on the otherwise unmodified USS ANTIETAM, CVA-36. This angled landing area was so successful that, on May 4, 1953, FORRESTAL's design was changed to incorporate it on a much larger scale than had been possible in ANTIETAM. The angled deck meant that any aircraft that missed the arresting cables would simply fly off of the angled portion of the deck and come around to try again rather than crash into barriers or other aircraft parked forward. It also meant that even the largest aircraft would be moving further and further away in a lateral direction from any island structure that the carrier might have on the starboard side. Therefore, the retractable island originally planned for FORRESTAL was eliminated long before construction had progressed that far, and it was replaced with a more conventional fixed superstructure. This simplified routing the intake and exhaust ducting to and from the funnel. Angled or canted landing decks have been on all subsequent U. S. carriers, and were added during conversions of all three MIDWAY class carriers and many of the ESSEX class ships.

By deciding to include a fixed superstructure, the starboard waist catapult had to be moved to a location next to the one on the port side. It was positioned at as much of an angle to the adjacent catapult as strength considerations for the flight deck would allow. This was done to permit positioning an aircraft on each of these catapults at the same time. Locating the inboard waist catapult slightly forward of the outboard one also helped make this possible. However, both of the waist catapults could not be fired at the same time as would have been possible if one had been located on each side as originally planned. This was a small consequence when compared to the advantages gained by the angled landing deck and the fixed superstructure.

Another British development was the steam catapult,

and it was also chosen for installation in FORRESTAL and all subsequent U. S. carriers. Far more capable than the former hydraulic catapults, and having substantial advantages over the black powder catapults being considered by the U. S. Navy, the steam catapults were another development that came along at exactly the right time for the super carrier. As completed, FORRESTAL had two C-11 steam catapults forward, and two C-7 steam catapults in the waist positions.

Another less noticeable development was the mirror landing aid that was used by pilots to properly line up their landing approaches. Using a mirror and a series of lights, this device replaced the landing signal officer's hand-held paddles that had guided so many aircraft to safe carrier landings. The landing signal officers remained on the LSO platform on the aft port side of the flight deck as they still do today, but with the mirror landing aid, they had moved into the electronic age. The mirror landing aid has since been replaced with the fresnel lens system.

With the changes incorporating an angled deck, fixed superstructure, and the locations of the four steam catapults made to the design plans, work progressed on FORRESTAL until she was christened and launched on December 11, 1954. It was Mrs. James V. Forrestal, widow of the late Secretary of Defense, who broke the ceremonial bottle of champagne across the bow of the new carrier just before she was launched. But there was still much work to do before the ship was completed. This included the addition of guns, elevators, catapults, radars, and other equipment. It would be October 1, 1955, before FORRESTAL became a commissioned ship of the U. S. Navy.

Prior to FORRESTAL, each class of aircraft carriers had represented a single step over the previous class in the evolutionary development of carriers that had dated back to the old LANGLEY. But with FORRESTAL's many new features, her design was much more than a single step over the previous MIDWAY class as built. Radical changes and improvements had been made in almost

Text continues on page 10.

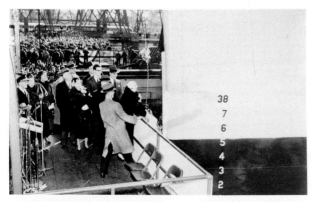

Mrs. James V. Forrestal breaks the ceremonial bottle of champagne on FORRESTAL's bow as the ship is christened on December 11, 1954. (National Archives)

After launching, tugs gently move FORRESTAL away from the drydock to another location where work on her construction will continue. (National Archives)

FORRESTAL's final form is visible in this photograph. Note how the superstructure was constructed nearer to the centerline than its final and permanent location would be. Once the basic structure was completed, it was moved to starboard and attached to the flight deck. *(National Archives)*

Now ready for sea, FORRESTAL gets up steam for the first time. Note that the catapult overruns on the bow have not been completed, but otherwise, the ship appears ready for operational service. *(National Archives)*

Underway for the first time, FORRESTAL heads down the Elizabeth River to begin her builder's trials. The catapults and arresting gear are clearly visible in this photograph.
(National Archives)

More details of FORRESTAL's flight deck are visible in this view. Note that the horizontal surfaces of the gun sponson are the same dark blue-gray as the flight deck. The FJ-3 Fury on cat one is piloted by CDR Ralph L. Werner, and is about to become the first aircraft launched from FORRESTAL. Shortly before this photograph was taken on January 3, 1956, CDR Werner had made the first arrested landing aboard FORRESTAL. *(National Archives)*

Now in operational service with the Navy, FORRESTAL shows off some of the early jet aircraft that operated from her deck. Banshees, Skyknights, Furies, Cutlasses, and Skyraiders are visible on deck. Note the completed catapult overruns as compared to the photographs on page 9. *(National Archives)*

every conceivable area, and FORRESTAL would become the basis for all subsequent U. S. carrier designs. Changes made since her design have been relatively minor when compared to those that differentiate her from all previous carrier designs.

By present standards, FORRESTAL's original electronics were uncomplicated and consisted of a small fraction of the number of today's systems. The primary radars included the SPS-8A, SPS-10, SPS-12, SPN-6, and SPN-8 systems. An ECM antenna was fitted to the aft mast, and fire control for the eight five-inch guns was supplied by four Mk 56 directors.

FORRESTAL's first commanding officer was Captain Roy L. Johnson, who took the ship to sea initially for short evaluation periods. During these early trials, CDR Ralph L. Werner landed an FJ-3 Fury on the ship's huge angled deck on January 3, 1956, thus becoming the first naval aviator to make an arrested recovery on a super carrier. He made the first launch from FORRESTAL using cat one that same day. Shortly thereafter, on January 24, 1956, the carrier began her shakedown cruise that lasted until March 28. After a brief yard period to correct deficiencies that had surfaced during her shakedown cruise, FORRESTAL returned to sea to begin conducting carrier qualifications.

In the fall of 1956, the Suez crisis erupted, and FORRESTAL was ordered to the Mediterranean with her commissioning crew still on board. Fortunately, the crisis was short lived, and the carrier was able to return home to Norfolk in time for the Christmas holidays.

Assigned to the Sixth Fleet, FORRESTAL began her first major deployment on January 23, 1957, as she departed Mayport, Florida, and headed toward the Medi-

DETAILS AS BUILT

The original flight deck markings can be seen in this overhead view. Landing lines and numbers are yellow, while most smaller lines are white. Markings around the elevators are red and yellow. Note the vertical supports for the two barricades just forward of the six arresting cables. Aircraft on the flight deck include A3D Skywarriors, F3H Demons, F9F Cougars, FJ-3 Furies, a C-1 Trader COD aircraft, and Piasecki HUP helicopters. *(National Archives)*

This port side view shows a lowered number two elevator, the original slanted stack, and the cutouts under the flight deck overhang with their small boarding decks. Notice the three small launches tied up under these decks. The original open fantail, a feature FORRESTAL shared with SARATOGA, is also apparent. RANGER and INDEPENDENCE had enclosed fantails. *(National Archives)*

Starboard side details of FORRESTAL as built are illustrated here. The two masts and slanted stack are again visible. The two large lattice antennas, located at the edge of the flight deck just aft of the superstructure, can be seen in the raised position. *(National Archives)*

The photograph above provides a good comparison of size and layout between FORRESTAL and the unmodified axial deck ESSEX class carrier VALLEY FORGE, CV-45. In the lower photograph, the FORRESTAL is moored next to the converted ESSEX class carrier INTREPID, CVA-11.
(Both National Archives)

Another comparison is shown here between FORRESTAL and the USS CORAL SEA, CVB-43, prior to the latter's conversion to an angled deck carrier. The three ships of the MIDWAY class, all completed ten years before FORRESTAL, were the largest carriers in the world prior to the FORRESTAL class and subsequent super carriers. The MIDWAY class carriers were the last built with axial decks and with centerline elevators. The CORAL SEA's two centerline elevators are seen in the lowered position in this photograph. These would later be replaced with deck edge elevators in subsequent conversions.   *(National Archives)*

terranean Sea. This cruise lasted until the carrier returned home on July 22. She then entered the Portsmouth Naval Yard for routine maintenance. After participating in the NATO exercise "Strikeback" and conducting a normal routine of qualifications and evaluations, FORRESTAL began her second major deployment to the Mediterranean on September 2, 1958. She returned to Norfolk the following March, and entered the yards for her first overhaul on April 1, 1959.

Although FORRESTAL's design was radically different from all previous carriers, only one major flaw had been found in her design during the first years she was in operation. This problem involved the arrangement of the elevators, and was primarily concerned with the fact that the location for the port side (number two) elevator made it almost useless during flight operations. It could not be used during landing operations, because it was part of the landing area, nor could it be used when aircraft were

This bow-on shot shows the five port holes for the secondary conning station in the bow, the two anchors, light units at the corners of the flight deck, and the bridle catchers or overruns for the catapults.

(National Archives)

Another view of the bow reveals more details of the catapult overruns and the supporting members under the catwalks.

(National Archives)

Details of the starboard side of the superstructure as built are shown here. The original slanted stack, two masts, and early radar fit are visible. The two bridges, one above the other, can be seen, and the auxiliary conning station is located just aft of the navigation bridge. Notice the lowered lattice antenna mast just forward of the number three elevator, and the details of the forward starboard gun sponson. Two A3D Skywarriors are positioned on the forward catapults with their wings and tails still in the folded position.

(National Archives)

being launched from the waist catapults. The only time it could be used during flight operations was when aircraft were being launched from only the two forward catapults and no other flight operations were taking place. The location of this elevator was inherited from former carrier designs, and by the time the problems associated with this location were realized, four ships of the class were far enough along in construction that moving the elevator was impractical. However, movement of the port side elevators to a position further aft was accomplished in MIDWAY and CORAL SEA in later conversions. The planned fifth and sixth ships of the FORRESTAL class were redesigned to correct the problem. The port side

elevator was moved to a location aft of the two waist catapults and out of the way of the landing area. This permitted its use during all flight operations. Additionally, the superstructure was moved aft so that two elevators were forward of its position and only one remained abaft it. This kept the elevators more spread out than would have been the case if the starboard arrangement had remained the same as it had been on the FORRESTAL class ships. The redesigned ships, beginning with CVA-63, formed the KITTY HAWK class of "improved FORRESTALs." This new layout for the elevators and the superstructure has remained the same on all subsequent U. S. carriers.

More details of the superstructure as built are visible in these two views. Details of the masts are also prominently displayed. In the photograph at left, a Banshee jet fighter gets the signal to launch from the catapult officer. The SPS-8A height finder radar is mounted forward on the superstructure above the bridges. At the top of the mast is the TACAN, and below it are SPS-10, SPS-12, and SPN-6 radar antennas. The aft mast has an ECM antenna at its head with a UHF/DF antenna below it. An SPS-8 radar is located under the small radome located at the base of and just aft of this mast. FORRESTAL and SARATOGA were the only two ships of the class to carry this second aft mast.

(Both National Archives)

Starboard side details are visible in this photograph taken while the ship replenished at sea. The original slanted smokestack has been replaced with a rectangular stack with a flat top. Again, note the darker blue-gray color of the horizontal surfaces.

(National Archives)

No other major problems were discovered with FORRESTAL, so changes were minor. The original slanted smoke stack was replaced with a rectangular one that had a flat top. The aft mast was changed to one that was T-shaped, and some of the smaller communications antennas were changed. An SPS-37 antenna was fitted to the forward lattice mast, and the aft lattice mast was replaced with a larger pole mast that also could be lowered during flight operations.

For the next two years, FORRESTAL continued a rigorous schedule of training, evaluating, and qualifying.

She made two more cruises to the Mediterranean Sea. In September 1961, she returned to the United States and entered the yards for a complete overhaul. The most noticeable change made during this yard period was the removal of her forward four five-inch guns, their sponsons, and their directors. The culprit that caused the removal of the guns was the sponson. The two forward sponsons crashed into heavy seas and slowed the ship's speed. They were also usually damaged in the process. Since the guns were considered to have only limited value against modern jet aircraft, their removal was

The original, yellow, converging, landing lines had been replaced by three, white, parallel lines when this photograph was taken on March 3, 1959. Aircraft on deck now include Skyhawks, Skyrays, Skywarriors, and Skyraiders. In fact, the only aircraft not built by Douglas Aircraft are the Vought Crusaders parked along the port side amidships. *(U. S. Navy)*

directed. The same was done to the other three ships in the class, except for RANGER, which retained the sponsons although the guns were removed. Her redesigned sponsons had proved less of a problem than on the three earlier ships of the class.

Another noticeable change made at this time was the addition of the large SPS-43 antenna on the starboard side of the island. To provide clearance for this radar, the aft T-shaped mast was raised to a height that was almost equal to the mainmast.

For the next few years, FORRESTAL alternated assignments between the Second Fleet in the Atlantic and the Sixth Fleet in the Mediterranean Sea. In November 1963, she conducted tests with the C-130 Hercules transport aircraft. Photographs taken during these tests can be found on page 18. Then, in April 1966, she began a major overhaul. It was during this yard period that she became the first carrier to receive the Naval

This overhead view shows the new flight deck markings used beginning in the 1958-59 time frame. The 59 at the aft end of the flight deck has been removed, and the one at the forward end is only an outline. In addition to the usual whip antennas, note the two T-shaped antennas lowered to starboard just forward of the five-inch gun mounts. *(U. S. Navy)*

Tactical Data System (NTDS). This sophisticated system allows the carrier to launch and recover aircraft electronically, and identify and track aircraft in her vicinity. It also is a control system that is more effective than previous systems at directing her own fighters to potentially hos-

Taken on February 13, 1960, this photograph shows the new flat or rectangular smokestack from the port quarter. Also notice that the aft mast has been changed from its original configuration. It is now T-shaped and has supports to the yardarm. This is the lower position for this T-shaped mast, and subsequent photographs will show it in a raised or higher position. In the background is FORRESTAL's sister ship, USS SARATOGA. This photograph was taken in Pollensa Bay, Majorca, 200 miles east of Valencia, Spain, while both carriers were operating with the Sixth Fleet.

(U. S. Navy)

tile aircraft. Although this major improvement to the ship's combat ability was not indicated with any significant external change, the dish-shaped SPS-30 antenna took the place of the SPS-8A forward on the superstructure. A dome covered another antenna at the aft end of her superstructure.

By the time this photograph was taken on January 22, 1962, the forward guns and their sponsons had been removed, leaving only four guns on the two aft sponsons. The forward sponsons had slowed the ship in heavy seas, and had been damaged on several occasions. Considering the lack of effectiveness of the five-inch guns against modern jet aircraft, the decision was made to remove them in order to save weight and allow for greater speed in rough seas.
(U. S. Navy)

The cleaner lines of the port side after the removal of the forward gun sponsons is illustrated here. Note the three solid landing lines. *(U. S. Navy)*

This front view again shows the effect of removing the forward gun sponsons. Note the addition of the SPS-43 radar antenna which has been mounted to the starboard side of the superstructure. To provide clearance, the aft T-shaped mast has been raised, and is now almost as tall as the foremast. *(U. S. Navy)*

C-130 TESTS

In November 1963, tests were conducted aboard FOR-RESTAL with the C-130 Hercules. A single, white, dashed, guide line was painted down the centerline of the ship as a reference for the pilot. The photographs at left and above show the C-130 positioned at the center of the flight deck. *(Both U. S. Navy)*

A humorous "LOOK MA, NO HOOK" was painted on the nose of the Hercules. *(U. S. Navy)*

These two photographs show the Hercules taking off from FORRESTAL without the assistance of a catapult. *(Both U. S. Navy)*

TRAGEDY IN THE GULF OF TONKIN

On July 29, 1967, while operating in the Gulf of Tonkin, and while preparing to launch a strike against targets in North Vietnam, an accident during flight operations caused a fire, explosions, and extensive damage to FORRESTAL's aft section. Here, the destroyer USS RUPERTUS, DD-851, stands by to assist FORRESTAL as smoke pours from the carrier.

(U. S. Navy)

Once FORRESTAL completed her yard period, she conducted the usual training and qualifications. Then, in June 1967, she departed Norfolk for a deployment to the Gulf of Tonkin off Vietnam. This would be her first, and as it turned out, last combat cruise. The first four days of air strikes against the North Vietnamese had been routine, and over 150 combat sorties had been flown by CVW-17. But at 1051 hours on July 29, 1967, fire broke out on the aft end of her flight deck. Fed by fuel from aircraft that were armed and ready for a strike, the fire spread quickly and several bombs exploded punching four large holes in the armored flight deck. Almost all of the aircraft parked aft of the superstructure were involved in the fire. Twenty-six were completely destroyed and thirty-one were damaged. The fire spread down through the holes in the deck, and more bombs fell through to the lower decks. Heroics on the part of the crew became commonplace as they fought the fires and carried armed bombs to the side and threw them overboard.

Once the fires were brought under control, the extent of the devastation became apparent. Most tragic was the loss of human life. A total of 134 crewmen were killed. Many died while heroically fighting the fires and trying to disarm bombs to save their ship. An additional 62 men were injured. Each year, on July 29, the present crew of FORRESTAL pauses to remember these men.

The damage to the ship was also extensive. With smoke still pouring from the carrier, she headed toward Cubi Point for initial repairs. In only eight days, repairs were made that would enable her to operate aircraft if necessary. She then continued her journey toward Norfolk for permanent repairs. Almost everything aft of her number four elevator and from the hangar deck up had to be rebuilt. Her four remaining five-inch guns were destroyed, and were removed. A swallow's nest was added to the starboard side forward, and on it was mounted a Mk 25 launcher for the Basic Point Defense Missile System (BPDMS). This remained the carrier's only defensive weapon system until 1976 when a second similar launcher was added to the port quarter. It was April 8, 1968, when FORRESTAL's repairs were completed, and she left the Norfolk Naval Shipyard ready to take her place in the fleet again.

These two photographs show crewmen as they fight the fires on the aft end of FORRESTAL's flight deck. The CAG's F-4 Phantom can be seen in the photograph at right. Almost all aircraft spotted aft of the superstructure were totally destroyed.

(Both U. S. Navy)

19

These two overhead views show the damage to the aft end of the ship after she arrived at Cubi Point, Philippines, on August 1, 1967.
(Both U. S. Navy)

The two aft guns on the starboard side are shown here after the fire. All four remaining guns were burned out and never replaced.
(U. S. Navy)

After returning to the Norfolk Naval Shipyard, most of FORRESTAL's aft section from the hangar deck up and from the number four elevator aft, had to be removed and rebuilt.
(U. S. Navy)

These two views further illustrate the extensive amount of work required to repair the carrier after the fire in the Gulf of Tonkin. Repairs were completed by April 8, 1968.
(Both U. S. Navy)

1968 TO THE PRESENT

After FORRESTAL was repaired and returned to duty, she looked like this. Note that the aft five-inch guns are gone as are the supporting structures that were beneath them. Only the base or lower portion of the gun sponson on the starboard quarter remains aft of the ship's crane. This is one distinguishing feature of FORRESTAL. Her sisters still have the supporting structures, but the guns have been removed. An early launcher (Mk 25) for the Sea Sparrow missile system has been installed in the position formerly occupied by the forward starboard gun sponson, but it is much smaller. No Phalanx gun systems had been installed when this photograph was taken in 1978. Although more cluttered than before, her fantail still remains open. The barrel-shaped items that have been added to the sides of the catwalks around the flight deck are self-inflating life rafts. *(U. S. Navy)*

Between 1968 and 1973, FORRESTAL made four deployments to the Mediterranean Sea. During a yard period in 1972, another physical change was made to her appearance in the form of a 120-foot long widening of her flight deck just aft of her number two elevator. This widening was necessitated because of safety requirements for new aircraft with a wider main landing gear than had been used before. In March 1973, during one of her deployments, she sped to Tunisia for rescue operations in the flooded Medjerda River Valley near Tunis. Her helicopters rescued hundreds of Tunisians during the three day operation, and transported thousands of pounds of food, water, and medical supplies to the stricken region. Three more deployments to the Mediterranean were logged between 1973 and 1975.

By 1976, Mk 28 Chaffroc systems were fitted. These

Also taken in 1978, this view shows FORRESTAL's port side. Again note the lack of Phalanx gun system. One would later be added just forward of the number two elevator, and another would be located aft near the fantail. The "angle on the angle," a small, 120-foot long widening of the flight deck just aft of the number two elevator on the port side, is barely visible. The aft mast is now just a stub, and the rectangular smoke stack has been raised.
(U. S. Navy)

The more enclosed fantail is visible in this view that was taken as FORRESTAL prepared to replenish at sea.

(FORRESTAL)

twin-tubed lauchers fired rockets that exploded clouds of chaff around the ship to confuse enemy radar signals. The major radar antennas included the large AN/SPS-43 "bedspring" antenna mounted to the starboard side of the island. A large dome on the aft end of the superstructure housed the NTDS and satellite communications antennas. Atop the forward end of the island was the SPS-30 air search and height finding dish antenna. The TACAN beacon was located at the head of the mast, and an SPS-58 low angle air search antenna was positioned about half way up the mast.

FORRESTAL was selected to be Host Ship for the International Naval Review in New York City. President Gerald Ford rang in the nations' bi-centennial celebration on July 4, 1976, and reviewed over forty "tall ships" from around the world from her deck.

Shortly after the review, FORRESTAL participated in a special shock test that involved the detonation of high explosives near the hull to determine if a capital ship could withstand the strain of close quarter combat and still remain operational.

In September 1977, following a nine month overhaul, FORRESTAL departed Norfolk and shifted her homeport to Mayport, Florida. After completing two more Mediterranean cruises, she celebrated her silver anniversary in October 1980. During 1980, the height of her smoke stack was increased ten feet.

In March 1981, FORRESTAL deployed to the Mediterranean Sea for the sixteenth time. It was during this cruise that the Syrian/Israeli missile crisis flared up, and FORRESTAL maintained a high state of readiness for fifty-three consecutive days at sea. Then in August 1981, during an exercise in the Gulf of Sidra, two Libyan Su-22s were shot down after firing on F-14s from VF-41 which was embarked in USS NIMITZ. FORRESTAL's aircraft made more than sixty percent of all intercepts of Libyan planes. She then departed the Mediterranean Sea to participate in the NATO exercise "Ocean Venture '81" above the Arctic Circle.

Her seventeenth Mediterranean cruise began on June 8, 1982. It was during this cruise that she operated in support of the contingency force of 800 U. S. Marines in Beirut, Lebanon. She transited the Suez Canal on September 12, 1982, and entered the Indian Ocean. This was the first time that she had operated with the Seventh Fleet since her 1967 cruise to Vietnam. On October 17, she transited the Suez Canal northbound and made a visit to Alexandria, Egypt.

Once she returned home in November, FORRESTAL began preparations for her major Service Life Extension Program (SLEP). She moved to the Philadelphia Navy Yard on January 18, 1983, to begin the twenty-eight month long program that was designed to extend her operational life fifteen to twenty years. During SLEP, FORRESTAL was emptied, and most major equipment was removed for rework or replacement. The Anti-Submarine Warfare (ASW) Tactical Support Center (TSC) was added during this period. Mk 29 launchers for the NATO Sea Sparrow missile system replaced the earlier Mk 25 launchers, and the associated radars were installed. Three Phalanx CIWS mounts were also added to the ship's defensive armament. The Mk 28 Chaffroc system was removed. Although the Mk 36 Rapid Bloom Offboard Chaff (RBOC) system is to be fitted, so far it has not been. FORRESTAL's SLEP cost over 550 million dollars, much more than twice the cost of building the ship in the early 1950s, but the increase in capabilities and the additional life added to the ship make these dollars far more cost effective than building a new carrier. Most present U. S. carriers have gone through the SLEP program, or are scheduled for it. This program will extend the life of all of these carriers, meaning fewer new carriers will have to be built. FORRESTAL's SLEP was completed on schedule on May 20, 1985, and she returned to her home port of Mayport, Florida. She immediately began the usual demanding workup schedule to prepare for her next major deployment. This continued until June 2, 1986, when FORRESTAL departed Mayport for her eighteenth deployment. During this cruise she operated near Libya, and also participated in operation "Sea Wind," a joint U. S./Egyptian training exercise. She then took part in "Display Determination" which featured low-level coordinated strikes and air combat maneuvering training over Turkey.

After returning home, FORRESTAL spent most of 1987 in yet another period of pre-deployment workups. This included refresher training, carrier qualifications, and a six week deployment to the North Atlantic to participate in "Ocean Safari '87." During this exercise she operated with other NATO forces in the fjords of Norway.

On April 28, 1988, FORRESTAL departed on her nineteenth major deployment. She steamed directly to the North Arabian Sea via the Suez Canal in support of America' s "Earnest Will" operations in the region. She spent 108 consecutive days at sea before her first liberty port. During the deployment, which lasted for five and one-half months, FORRESTAL operated in three ocean areas and spent only fifteen days in port. She returned on October 7, 1988, and received the Meritorious Unit Citation for her superior operational performance during the deployment.

After a brief but well deserved rest, FORRESTAL began preparing for her twentieth deployment. She sailed to New York City to participate in Fleet Week between April 29 and May 3, 1989. She then resumed preparations for her major deployment which began in October 1989. As this is written, she is still on that deployment, and is due back in April 1990. With twenty major deployments to her record, she remains the world's first super carrier, and "First in Defense" of America.

On the pages that follow is a close-up look at FORRESTAL's air wing and details of the ship as she appears today. Everything from her present radar fit to her weapons systems, from her bridges to her engine room, and from her catapults to her rudders is illustrated. Many of these photographs were chosen from over 2000 in order to give the reader an understanding for the many items, areas, and facets that comprise a super carrier. Others were chosen to provide a reference source from which scale modelers can detail models of FORRESTAL as she has appeared during different points in her operational career. Regardless of his or her reason for reading this book, the reader will find it the most detailed look at the USS FORRESTAL ever published.

This photograph shows FORRESTAL generally as she appears today. The Sea Sparrow launcher is a later version, and the Belknap or Kennedy pole mast has been added just aft of it.
(U. S. Navy)

CARRIER AIR WING SIX

F-14A TOMCAT SQUADRONS

VF-11 "RED RIPPERS"

This is the squadron commander's aircraft for the "Red Rippers" of VF-11, one of two F-14A Tomcat fighter squadrons assigned to Carrier Air Wing Six and USS FORRESTAL. The aircraft is painted in the overall light gull gray scheme, and has colorful tail markings. The national insignia is black. The nose number, called a modex, on VF-11's F-14s begins with a 1.

Another Tomcat from VF-11 is shown here in the tactical paint scheme. Markings are in various shades of gray.

VF-31 "TOMCATTERS"

The other Tomcat squadron aboard FORRESTAL is VF-31, which is known as the "Tomcatters." This is the CAG aircraft from VF-31, and it is adorned with colorful markings on the overall light gull gray scheme. The squadron is a descendant of the famous VF-3 from World War II, and uses the same Felix-the-Cat insignia. Tomcats assigned to this squadron have a modex beginning with the number 2.

Aircraft 210 is shown in the photograph at left, and is painted in the same scheme and markings as the CAG aircraft shown above. The AE tail code is visible on the inside of the tail. At right is number 206, which is painted in the tactical scheme. It has low visibility gray markings. About half of the Tomcats aboard FORRESTAL in July 1989 had returned to the more colorful markings shown at left. Both Tomcat squadrons are shore based at NAS Oceana, Virginia.

A-7E CORSAIR II SQUADRONS

Two attack squadrons fly the A-7E from FORRESTAL. One is VA-37, which is known as the "Bulls," and their Corsairs have nose numbers beginning with a 3. This is one of their aircraft shown taxiing forward and folding its wings after making an arrested landing. A FLIR pod and a Shrike missile can be seen attached to pylons under the right wing.

VA-37's markings are more easily seen in this view. Note the bull painted on the vertical tail.

VA-105 "GUNSLINGERS"

The second A-7E squadron is VA-105, which is nicknamed "Gunslingers." This is the CAG aircraft from VA-105, and an external fuel tank, Shrike missile, and multiple ejector rack can be seen under the left wing. Nose numbers beginning with a 4 are painted on VA-105's Corsairs.

VA-105's markings are better illustrated in these two views. All of the Corsairs in both squadrons are painted in the low visibility tactical scheme. Both VA-37 and VA-105 are shore based at NAS Cecil Field, Florida. FORRESTAL's A-7Es have not been replaced with the F/A-18 Hornet, because equipment aboard the ship has not been modified to operate the Hornet yet. These changes are scheduled to be made in 1992. Although F/A-18s were aboard during Fleet Week in 1990 when FORRESTAL visited New York, they were not part of the air wing.

A-6E INTRUDER & EA-6B PROWLER SQUADRONS

VA-176

"THUNDERBOLTS"

VA-176 is the all-weather attack squadron assigned to Carrier Air Wing Six, and it flies the A-6E TRAM Intruder. These aircraft are painted in the tactical paint scheme with gray and black markings. They have nose numbers beginning with a 5.

At left is another Intruder shown just after landing. At right is a KA-6D tanker aircraft which is also assigned to VA-176. The tankers are painted in the light gull gray over white scheme, and have more colorful markings. VA-176 is shore based at NAS Oceana, Virginia.

VAQ-142 "GRIM WATCH DOGS"

The EA-6B Prowler electronic warfare version of the A-6 design is flown by VAQ-142. All EA-6B squadrons are based at NAS Whidbey Island, Washington. These two photographs show two of the Prowlers assigned to the "Grim Watch Dogs." Note that the modex on these aircraft begins with a 6. All of the squadron's EA-6Bs are painted in the tactical scheme with low visibility markings.

E-2C HAWKEYE SQUADRON

VAW-122 "STEELJAWS"

The "Steeljaws" of VAW-122 fly the E-2C Hawkeye all-weather early warning and control aircraft from FORRESTAL. Like VAQ-142, the nose numbers on VAW-122's aircraft begin with a 6. In this photograph, the JBD is already raised behind the aircraft as E-2C number 601 carefully inches forward on to cat two.   (Head)

The E-2C is often called the "Hummer." Here, number 602 folds its wings after landing, and prepares to taxi forward to its parking spot. Note the unusual AJ code on the wing instead of the AE that is the proper code for CVW-6.

S-3A VIKING SQUADRON

VS-28 "GAMBLERS"

VS-28 is known as the "Gamblers," and they fly the S-3A Viking anti-submarine warfare ASW aircraft. Most of these aircraft are painted in the light gull gray over white scheme with low visibility markings, although some S-3As are painted in the tactical scheme. Nose numbers begin with a 7. At left is number 703 touching down on FORRESTAL, and at right is number 710 as it taxies to the catapult for launch.
(Left FORRESTAL, right author)

SH-3H SEA KING SQUADRON HS-15 "RED LIONS"

The "Red Lions" of Helicopter Anti-submarine Squadron Fifteen, HS-15, fly the SH-3H version of the Sea King. Their helicopters have numbers beginning with a 6. Here 611 takes off to fly orbits off of the starboard side of the ship while flight operations take place. In the event of an accident, they will rush to the scene to rescue crewmen.

HS-15 also performs the anti-submarine mission, and moves personnel and cargo between ships at sea and between the ship and the shore. At left, 610 is refueled between missions, and at right 611 is shown parked on the flight deck with its rotors and tail section folded for storage. These helicopters are painted in the tactical scheme with low visibility markings.

When the entire air wing is aboard the ship, aircraft are crowded into every available inch of space. Only about twenty-eight aircraft can be in the hangar bays, so most of the aircraft are kept on the flight deck. Here, aircraft are spotted forward, leaving the landing area open to recover aircraft if necessary. Additionally, aircraft can be launched from the waist catapults when aircraft are spotted as shown here. Therefore, the carrier remains able to conduct flight operations even when this many aircraft are on the flight deck.

FORRESTAL DETAILS
MAST & PRIMARY RADARS

The AN/SPS-48 radar antenna is located forward on the superstructure.

At the top of the mast is the AS-3240/URN TACAN antenna. The larger radar to the right in the photograph (mounted aft and to port on the mast) is the SPN-43 radar antenna which is used for low-level, close-in air search. The radar mounted low and forward on the mast, just above the AN/SPS-48, is the Mk 48 Mod 1 antenna that is used for the target acquisition system.

The mast is shown from behind in this photograph. The aft mast supports various wire antennas. Almost every small dome, pole, and dish is an antenna of some kind. There are literally dozens of antennas of all types located on the superstructure. The white dome in the lower right corner of the photograph houses the SEATEL antenna, while the dish antenna beside it is for the SPN-42 which is associated with the automatic carrier landing system. The smaller dish below pri-fly is the SPN-44 that measures the airspeed of incoming aircraft as they approach the carrier for landing.

This view shows the AN/SPS-49 radar antenna from behind. It is used for long range air search. ECM antennas are attached to its supporting sponson.

SUPERSTRUCTURE

The superstructure is shown from the front in this view. Two long 4-12 MHz fiberglass whip antennas are mounted above the bridges and angle forward from the superstructure.

More details of the starboard side of the superstructure are shown here. The white dome of the Phalanx close-in weapon system (CIWS) is clearly visible at the center of the island. The 59 painted on the island is difficult to see on this side due to the numerous louvers cut into the metal.

More details of the island are seen in this photograph taken from behind. Numerous speakers and floodlights can be seen mounted around the upper levels.

Here is the superstructure from the port side. The lower areas on this side, and on the front and rear, are painted black. The large rectangular smoke stack is also painted flat black, as is the upper portion of the masts and radars.

Shapes and supporting members for the various platforms and sponsons on the starboard side of the superstructure are shown here. Note the shape of the auxiliary conning station that is located aft of the two bridges. The platform just below the bridges is for a man armed with Stinger shoulder-fired air defense missiles.

High atop the superstructure, a crewman signals FOR-RESTAL's sister ship, USS SARATOGA, during exercises off the Florida coast in July 1989.

Details of the larger rectangular stack are shown here. Two SPS-49 antennas protrude from the top of the stack, while a 10-30 MHz trussed whip antenna is located just aft and to port of it.

These two views show the flag boxes on each side of the island. At left is the one on the port side, and is shown uncovered. At right is the starboard flag box, which was covered when this photograph was taken.

Inside the superstructure at the flight deck level is the flight deck control center. An outline of the flight deck is marked on the clear plastic top of the table, and scale representations of the aircraft types are positioned on it just as the real aircraft are positioned on the flight deck. Aircraft spotting is continually plotted and managed from this point.   (USS FORRESTAL)

BRIDGES

FORRESTAL has two bridges located one above the other at the forward end of the superstructure. The top one is the navigation bridge, and the lower one is the flag bridge. At left is a view of the bridges from the front, and at right is a view from the port side. Note how the navigation bridge extends further aft on this side.

This view shows the bridges from the starboard side. At the aft end of the navigation bridge is the auxiliary conning station.

This is the interior of the navigation bridge as viewed from the port side and looking forward and to starboard. The engine order telegraph is in the foreground, and the ship's wheel is just beyond that. Both are covered in polished brass.

The interior of the flag bridge is shown here. The view was taken in the forward corner on the starboard side, and looks to port. The admiral's chair can be seen in the background.

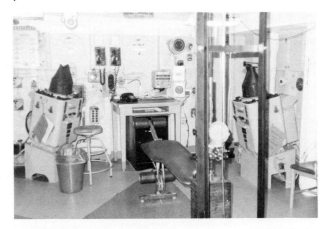

Just inside of the flag bridge is this room which has radar scopes and an exercise station.

COLOR GALLERY

Taken on November 12, 1959, this photograph shows FORRESTAL basically in her original configuration. The original slanted smoke stack has been replaced with the rectangular one, and the T-shaped aft mast has been substituted for the earlier one. The aft lattice mast on the starboard side has been replaced with a pole mast that is shown here in the lowered position. The forward lattice mast remains, but is now topped with a SPS-37 antenna. Otherwise, the ship appears to be in her "as built" appearance, and she still retains her forward five-inch gun mounts.   (U. S. Navy)

FORRESTAL is shown here in March 1964, while she was operating in the Caribbean Sea with her full air group on board. The higher aft T-mast is clearly visible.   (U. S. Navy)

Both of these photographs were taken on January 9, 1967, and show FORRESTAL as she appeared at the time of her tragic fire off Vietnam in July of that year. Her aft five-inch mounts are still in place, and although an engine test stand and a landing aid have been added to her fantail, it is still basically open. The aft mast is now completely gone.

(Both U. S. Navy)

This photograph was taken on August 12, 1967, as FOR-RESTAL steamed back to the United States after her fire off Vietnam. Temporary repairs made at Cubi Point made it possible for the carrier to operate aircraft if necessary. Patches over the holes in the flight deck are clearly visible. The burned out guns and damaged fantail are also evident in this stern view. (U. S. Navy)

This photograph, and the two below, show FORRESTAL as she appeared on April 8, 1968. She is being moved out of the Norfolk Naval Shipyard after extensive work was done to repair the damage to her aft section that was caused by the fire and explosions that occurred off Vietnam the previous July. The new areas of the aft flight deck are clearly visible. Note that all five-inch guns are now gone, and a Mk 25 Sea Sparrow missile launcher has been installed forward on the starboard side. (U. S. Navy)

Taken in 1971, this photograph shows FORRESTAL back in action with her air group on board. (U. S. Navy)

FORRESTAL is shown here during her SLEP overhaul. Note the primer red paint on the superstructure. The ship was virtually rebuilt at this time, and the Phalanx gun system was added. (USS FORRESTAL)

FORRESTAL is shown here as she exits the Suez Canal during her 1988 deployment. The 108 spelled out on the deck by her crewmen is to indicate that the ship had spent 108 consecutive days at sea. *(USS FORRESTAL)*

From April 29 until May 3, 1989, FORRESTAL visited New York City for Fleet Week. F/A-18 Hornets from VFA-81 and VFA-83 were embarked for the visit, but are not a part of the air group. *(USS FORRESTAL)*

FORRESTAL, seen here in the foreground, is shown with the NIMITZ class nuclear powered carrier USS THEODORE ROOSEVELT. By comparison, note how much further aft the superstructure is on the ROOSEVELT. The supporting structure for the flight deck overhang is far more streamlined, and this is made possible because the port elevator is at the aft end of the overhang rather than at the forward end. Because there is no smoke stack on the nuclear powered carriers, and because there is a radar mast aft of the island, the superstructure can be smaller than those found on the FORRESTAL class carriers. At the time this photograph was taken in 1988, FORRESTAL was the oldest, and ROOSEVELT the newest of the Navy's super carriers. *(USS FORRESTAL)*

These three photographs were taken by the author as FORRESTAL operated off the Florida coast in July 1989. In this photograph, launch operations are about to begin as handlers start moving aircraft toward the catapults.

In these two views launch operations are complete, as indicated by the fact that the flight deck is far less cluttered with aircraft. Planes that remain are being respotted for recovery. These views, along with those on the covers, show details of the ship as she appears today.

As flight operations begin for the evening launch, an A-7E from VA-37 moves forward to cat one. The deck crewman holding up the black box-like device is checking the weight of the aircraft with the pilot. The box has a weight on it that the pilot can see. If it is correct for his aircraft, he signals his approval to the crewman. If not, he has it adjusted until the proper weight is displayed. This weight is then used to set the proper amount of steam pressure for the catapult. *(Head)*

S-3A 704 moves forward toward the catapults and unfolds its wings in the process. All movement of aircraft on the flight deck is carefully controlled by deck crewmen. *(Head)*

An A-6E TRAM taxis over the JBD behind cat one, and receives a visual inspection from crewmen. Small practice bombs are attached to the multiple ejector rack. *(Head)*

Inching forward with its catapult launch arm lowered, an A-7E is about to engage cat two. *(Head)*

Hooked up and ready to go, an E-2C runs up its engines and completes its pre-launch checks. *(Head)*

Crewmen give an A-7E a good looking over just prior to launch on cat three. Note the smaller JBD behind cat three in the raised position. A Walleye glide bomb is attached under the wing of the Corsair. An F-14 Tomcat is being positioned on cat four in the background. (Head)

This EA-6B Prowler is disengaging the arresting cable after making a successful recovery. The arresting gear pulls the aircraft backwards slightly, leaving it clear of the arresting cable as shown here. The pilot then retracts the tail hook and taxies forward.

This S-3A Viking is caught in midair as it passes the superstructure while making a touch-and-go landing. (Head)

SH-3H 610 goes through its pre-flight checks prior to starting its engines. HS-15 is a busy squadron, flying orbits near the ship while all flight operations are being conducted, and performing the anti-submarine mission as well. The versatile helicopters can be called on to accomplish a variety of other missions as well.

Air operations must be carefully orchestrated so that they can be conducted in such a way that there will also be enough room to park aircraft. An S-3A is shown just prior to launch from cat one, while an A-7E unfolds its wings behind the JBD. Once the Viking has departed, the Corsair will make a hard right turn to position on the cat. Aircraft that have just landed are being parked forward at the end of cat two. Others are being taken below on the elevators.

The pilot of an EA-6B checks the movement of his control surfaces as one of the final checks just prior to launching from cat four.

Between flight operations, aircraft are respotted for the next launch or recovery. An A-7E Corsair is being moved aft in this view. Deck crewmen work almost around the clock, even when flight operations are not underway.

Here, an S-3A Viking is being backed out of its parking spot forward on the flight deck and . . .

. . . is respotted well aft on the flight deck. Aircraft are spotted clear of the catapults so that they will be ready to use for the next launch.

PRI-FLY

Pri-fly is the primary flight control station for the ship. In layman's terms, it is the carrier's control tower. On FORRESTAL it is located at the aft end of the superstructure. The photograph on the left shows pri-fly as viewed from the port side, and at right is a view from aft of the island. Note the small enclosed area just below pri-fly which houses a television camera used for recording flight operations.

These two photographs were taken inside pri-fly. The view on the left looks forward from the entrance, and the view at right looks aft from the forward-most point of pri-fly.

This photo looks to port from the entrance, and reveals the interior of that portion of pri-fly that extends out the most over the flight deck. Chairs for the air boss and mini boss are visible in this area. When flight operations are in progress, pri-fly is jammed with people, making photography almost impossible. Therefore, these photographs were taken while the ship was in port.

CATAPULTS

Ever since jet aircraft began to operate from aircraft carriers, there has been a need for strong catapults and jet blast deflectors (JBDs) to deflect the jet's exhaust as the engines are run up to full take-off power. When FORRESTAL was built, she was equipped with JBDs seen in these two photographs. One of these JBDs was behind cats one, two, and three. There was no need for a JBD behind cat four since the exhaust simply went off the edge of the deck. These original JBDs were stored flush in the deck. When needed for launch, they were raised, then rotated ninety degrees behind the aircraft. At left is a photograph of a Crusader at the moment of launch, with the JBD in the raised and rotated position. At right the JBD behind cat two can be seen in the lowered position just beyond the vertical tail of the Fury. When lowered, the JBD's position was an interesting pattern of red and yellow striped lines. The JBD behind cat one can be seen in the raised position. It is being rotated so that it can be lowered into the deck to allow the Fury to taxi into the position for launching.

(Both National Archives)

The earlier JBDs soon gave way to ones similar to those installed today. These JBDs are much larger, and are hinged at the forward end. They lie flush with the deck until the aircraft is positioned on the cat for launch. They are then raised behind the aircraft to deflect the exhaust up and over crewmen and aircraft behind the catapult. At left, a KA-6D taxies over the JBD behind cat one as it moves forward on to the catapult. At right, the JBD is shown raised behind an F-14 as it prepares to launch.

This close-up view shows the JBD behind cat two from behind. JBDs are water cooled so that they can stand the terrific heat from jet exhausts. The three longer and lighter colored braces are placed behind the JBD's sections during maintenance or inspection, but are not present during operations.

The JBD behind cat three is smaller than the other two, and is shown here in the lowered position. Because of the arrangement of the catapults on FORRESTAL class carriers, there is still no need for a JBD behind cat four as there is on all subsequent classes of U. S. carriers.

When FORRESTAL was commissioned, aircraft used a series of bridles and cables for launch. The bridle can be seen hooked to this A-4 Skyhawk. A hold-back cable was attached between the aft section of the aircraft and the deck. When the catapult was fired, a breakable bolt in this holdback cable broke, and the bridle pulled the aircraft along the catapult for launch. Several of the bridles and cables can be seen in the foreground. *(U. S. Navy)*

The bolts to the holdback cables were placed in these cleats in the flight deck. The type of aircraft being launched would determine which cleat would be used.

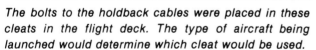

Two catapult overruns or bridle catchers were positioned forward of cats one and two. The bridle used for launching the aircraft would be stopped by cables that extended down the entire length of the catapult and on to these overruns. Only the bridle catcher on cat one is now used, since very few aircraft use the bridle system anymore.

Almost all of today's carrier-based aircraft use the nose wheel tow system. An arm, that is attached to the nose wheel strut, is positioned into the catapult as shown here. The holdback bar is also attached to the nose wheel strut, and can be seen just to the right of the crewman who is positioning the aircraft on the catapult. *(U. S. Navy)*

This photograph shows the nose wheel tow system in operation as an F-14 Tomcat is pulled by the catapult for launch. This photograph was taken aboard FORRESTAL while the Tomcat went through carrier suitability trials in November 1973. *(U. S. Navy)*

CATS ONE & TWO

With the JBD raised behind it, an A-7E from VA-105 is readied for launch on cat two.

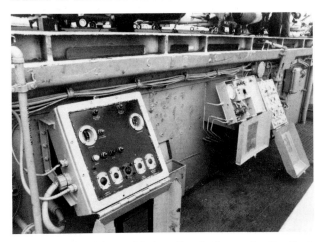

Cat two is fired from this location in the port catwalk. A similar firing console is located in the starboard catwalk for cat one.

The correct amount of steam pressure is ordered from this position located between the two forward catapults. The amount of pressure required depends on the weight of the aircraft being launched.

This view looks along cat two from the forward-most end. An E-2C Hawkeye is positioned on the catapult at the other end. Note how cat two now stops short of the end of the flight deck instead of continuing on to the bridle catcher. Compare the forward ends of cats one and two as shown in the overhead views on the front and rear covers.

Crewmen perform maintenance on cat one as the carrier steams toward its home port of Mayport, Florida.

Both cats three and four are fired from positions in the port catwalk adjacent to the catapults.

This is cat three as viewed from behind. The guide for positioning the launch arm is not on the catapult as it is in the bottom left photograph of cat four.

The position where the steam is ordered for cats three and four is located between the two catapults, and is the same as the one for cats one and two shown on the previous page.

At left is cat four as viewed from the aft end, while at right is the same catapult as seen from the forward end. In the photograph at left, the guide used to assist the nose wheel launch arm into position can be seen on the catapult.

LANDING AREA & ARRESTING GEAR

When FORRESTAL was commissioned, she had six arresting cables and two barricades. She now has four cables and only one barricade. This photograph shows the CAG A-7E from VA-105 as it engages one of the cables on landing.

(USS FORRESTAL)

Taken many years earlier on April 5, 1963, this photo shows the smoking tires of an A-5 Vigilante as the tail hook engages a wire to bring the aircraft to a stop in two seconds.

(U. S. Navy)

As the arresting gear brings this E-2C to a stop, its nose gear is on elevator number two. With this elevator positioned in the landing area and forward of cats three and four, it becomes clear why this elevator cannot be used during most flight operations. It cannot be used at any time arrested recoveries are taking place. Note that the arresting cable is still attached to the tail hook of the aircraft.

One of the retractable fair lead sheaves is shown in this view. The cross-deck pendant (that part of the cable that stretches across the deck between the two fair lead sheaves) has been removed from the purchase cable, which is that part of the cable that runs down to the arresting gear engines below the deck.

This photograph was taken down in one of the arresting gear engine rooms. There are four such rooms, one for each cable.

At left is a fair lead sheave in the retracted position. Its top is flush with the flight deck. The cross-deck pendant is attached to the purchase cable at a junction called a terminal. The terminal is clearly visible in this photograph. At right is a sheave in the extended position as it would be while aircraft are recovering.

These two views show one of the fair lead sheaves being disassembled for maintenance between flight operations.

Cross-deck pendants are held up off of the flight deck by simple, flat, leaf springs as shown here.

When an aircraft engages the cable, the terminal impacts on the flight deck, and can cause damage to both the deck and the terminal. Therefore, rectangular impact pads are positioned on the flight deck as shown in this view. There are two pads for each cable, one at each end.

In any emergency when a normal arrested recovery cannot be made, a barricade can be erected in about two minutes time. This barricade, specifically designed for jet aircraft, is stored under the flight deck beneath the outlined cover shown at left. At right is the erected barricade.

(Left author, right U. S. Navy)

ELEVATORS

Elevator number one is the elevator located forward of the island on the starboard side. Here, the elevator is in the raised position. When not in use moving aircraft between decks, the elevators are usually in the raised position, and are part of the parking area for aircraft.

More details of elevator number one are visible in this view taken while the ship was in port.

Elevator number two is the only elevator on the port side. It is almost always in the raised position since it is part of the landing area and part of the take-off area for catapults three and four. The markings around the elevator can be seen from this photograph that was taken from the superstructure.

This photograph shows elevator number one in the lowered position. An F-14 Tomcat is being moved forward off of the elevator and into the hangar bay.

This view of elevator number one was taken from the top of the superstructure, and shows an F7U Cutlass being moved on to the hangar deck. Numerous details can be seen to include the red and orange markings around and on the elevator, the double oval opening in the side of the hull that leads to the hangar bay, the retractable fence on the flight deck that raises when the elevator is down, and some of the cables which help raise and lower the elevator. This early photograph was taken before the deck just forward of the lowered elevator was lengthened forward to form FORRESTAL's larger quarterdeck. (U. S. Navy)

This view shows the opening in the hull for the number two elevator. The large guides for the elevator can be seen on either side of the opening.

Elevator number three is the one located just aft of the superstructure on the starboard side. In this view, the elevator is shown in the up position, and it is being used as part of the parking area for the F-14s. The doors leading to the hangar bay are closed, and crates of supplies are positioned between the doors and the edge of the hull. The refueling deck is forward of the opening, and a boat deck is located aft of it. Refueling apparatus is also located on this deck.

This is elevator number four, which is the aft-most elevator on the starboard side. Much cargo passes over this elevator when the carrier is in port, because the ship's crane (not visible in this photo) is located just aft of it. The crane can hoist items on to and off of the lowered elevator.

This view shows the supporting structure underneath one of the elevators. This structure is common to all four elevators.

Elevator number three is shown here in the lowered position, and a large gangway has been placed on it while the ship is in port. Note the holes in the side of the elevator.

This is elevator number four as seen while the ship was at sea. All of FORRESTAL's elevators are rectangular in shape and measure 63 X 52 feet in size. Elevators on all U. S. carriers built after the FORRESTAL class have a triangular-shaped addition on their outer edge that increases their area.

Taken from the aft end of the hangar bay opening for elevator number four and looking forward, this view shows the cross section of the oval opening that is common to all elevators. There are actually two oval openings, one inside the other, and they are separated by a flat vertical wall.

FLIGHT DECK WALK-AROUND

Four saluting guns are mounted in the forward catwalks. These are on the port side. The ringed mount between the guns is a firing position for a gunner armed with a Stinger, shoulder-fired, air defense missile. The camera just aft of the guns is an infrared camera that photographs landing aircraft from the head-on position.

These are the starboard side saluting guns. The Belknap pole is located outboard of these guns, and another Stinger mount is located on its supporting sponson.

All aircraft carriers in the U. S. Navy, with the exception of the USS LEXINGTON, have been fitted with a tall pole mast that is located forward on the starboard side. Known as the Belknap or Kennedy pole, it has a navigation light at its head, and provides more distance between this light and the one at the head of the main mast than previously possible. This is an aid to navigation at night, and helps other ships determine which direction the carrier is heading. Since the superstructure of an aircraft carrier is so short in relation to its overall length, without this pole mast there is not enough distance between these two navigation lights to allow other ships to accurately determine the direction in which the carrier is heading. Reportedly, this was a contributing factor in the collision between the cruiser USS BELKNAP and the carrier USS JOHN F. KENNEDY. Therefore, these poles were fitted to the carriers and named Belknap or Kennedy poles. The photo at left was taken from in front of the pole, and the photo at right was taken from a position aft of the pole.

This view looks forward along the port catwalk that runs along the forward end of the flight deck. The photograph was taken from the number two elevator. Hoses for numerous aircraft refueling and fire fighting stations can be seen on their reels. Such stations are found in the catwalks all around the flight deck.

The ship's bell is located at the forward-most point of the catwalk on the starboard side.

At various positions around the flight deck are locations that provide electrical power for aircraft. At left, one of these positions is shown closed, and at right, another power source is opened up. A power cable is pulled from the location and connected to the aircraft.

Part of the OT-32/SPN-41 automatic landing control radar is sponsored out to port as seen in these two views. This portion of the system is the elevation dome, while the azimuth dome is located on the fantail.

LSO PLATFORM

The LSO platform is located aft on the port side of the flight deck as it is on all U. S. aircraft carriers. At left is a view of FORRESTAL's LSO platform as viewed from a position aft of the platform and looking forward. The photograph at right shows the HUD in the closed and retracted position, and the console with its cover in place.

A shield to protect the LSOs from the wind over the deck (WOD) is mounted on the LSO platform. It has four windows to allow the LSOs to see forward. In the photograph at right, the netting around the platform can be seen. In the event of an emergency, the LSOs can jump into this netting and slide down under the platform.

Crewmen are shown here erecting the HUD and preparing it for use.

Details of the console are shown here.

MIRROR LANDING AID & FRESNEL LENS

When FORRESTAL entered service, the mirror landing aid was used to assist pilots in lining up their approaches to the carrier. It was mounted on a mobile unit, and was usually placed to the starboard side of the landing area as seen here. This photograph was taken as a Douglas F4D Skyray made its approach to the carrier. (National Archives)

Details of the business end of a mirror landing aid can be seen here. Notice the distorted reflection of a helicopter in the mirror. (National Archives)

The mirror landing aid is shown again in this photo that was taken while Vought's F8U Crusader underwent carrier suitability trials. (National Archives)

The mirror landing aid gave way to the fresnel lens system used today. This is the fresnel lens as viewed from a position aft of its mount. The shield forward of the lens system is painted black on its aft side to provide a good contrast for the lights.

This is the forward side of the fresnel lens system.

This photograph was taken even with the lens, and looks to port across the top of the system and its supporting platform.

HANGAR DECK

FORRESTAL's hangar deck is 75,000 square feet in area, and can accommodate about twenty-eight aircraft. It can be divided into three bays by large fireproof and blastproof doors. More involved maintenance can be performed on the hangar deck than on the flight deck. Crewmen are shown here working on one of VF-11's F-14 Tomcats near the forward end of the hangar deck.

This is the forward end of the hangar deck, and part of the opening for elevator number two can be seen at left. It can be seen here that the hangar deck does not extend forward of the numbers one and two elevators.

This view was taken from a point about even with the number three elevator, and looks forward.

Aircraft are usually moved to the sides of the hangar deck for maintenance, keeping the center area free to move other planes. But at times, every square inch is taken up with parked aircraft. At left is an S-3A Viking undergoing maintenance. Note how its tail folds down for clearance. The overhead in the hangar bays is twenty-five feet above the deck. At right is an A-7E Corsair II undergoing checks. Note how external fuel tanks are suspended along the sides of the hangar bays.

These crewmen are about to perform an engine change on an A-7E.

During replenishment at sea, supplies of all types are moved from the supply ship, across the lowered starboard elevators, and into the hangar bays. They are then lowered to the appropriate holds within the ship. At left a large supply of soft drinks awaits its trip on the elevator, while at right, cherry tomatoes, peaches, and other food supplies are stacked and waiting to be moved to the food storage lockers.

With the elevator door in the open position and the elevator at the hangar deck level, supplies are being sent to their proper storage areas within the ship.

The ship's boats are stored at the aft end of the hangar deck.

STARBOARD SIDE DETAILS

Details of the starboard bow are shown here.

FORRESTAL's quarterdeck is located just forward of the number one elevator at the hangar deck level. It is here that officers and visiting VIPs board and depart the carrier.

The supporting structure and overhang on which the superstructure is mounted is shown here. A portion of the lowered number one elevator can be seen to the right in this photo.

The refueling deck is located just aft of the supporting structure seen at left, and is just forward of the number three elevator.

This deck is between the numbers three and four elevators. A whaleboat can be seen to the right, with the words "GO NAVY" spelled out above it. More refueling hoses are on the aft end of this deck. Supporting booms for these hoses are attached to the flight deck overhang.

The ship's crane is located just aft of the number four elevator. The mounts for the former five-inch guns have been removed from the large sponson aft of the crane, but remain on the other ships of the FORRESTAL class. Note that there is no Sea Sparrow launcher mounted on this quarter.

This is the fantail area as viewed from the starboard side.

PORT SIDE DETAILS

Photographing the starboard side of a carrier is usually fairly easy, because carriers berth with their starboard side to the pier. Photographing the port side usually requires a flight in a helicopter or other aircraft, or a trip in a boat! These detailed photograph of FORRESTAL's port side were taken from one of HS-15's helicopters. At left is the port bow. The anchor and lowered fiberglass whip antennas can be seen in this view. At right, details of the Phalanx gun mount and part of the opening for the number two elevator are visible.

Moving further aft, more details of the port side can be seen. Note the ECM antennas just aft of the number two elevator, the lowered whip antennas, and the small enclosed deck below the overhang.

The aft end of the flight deck overhang is shown here. Two more small decks are sponsoned out from the ship at the hangar deck level, and cutouts are made into the overhang above them. The elevation dome for the SPN-41 radar can be seen just to the left of the tail of the closest Tomcat.

The entire port quarter is shown in this view. The Sea Sparrow launcher and its two associated radars are visible, as is the Phalanx mount that is located at the extreme aft end of the port side. The black LSO platform can be seen between and above the Sea Sparrow launcher and its radars.

ANCHORS & FOC'SLE

FORRESTAL has two anchors, each weighing thirty tons. One is located on each side of her bow in a conventional arrangement. This differs from what is seen on some carriers that have an anchor mounted forward on the bow on a stem hawespipe. Such was the case on AMERICA covered in D&S volume 34. This head-on view shows the location of both anchors to good effect. *(USS FORRESTAL)*

Details of the starboard anchor are shown here.

This is the port side anchor. When this photograph was taken, the anchor was not pulled all the way back into its hole. *(USS FORRESTAL)*

This view was taken in the fos'cle, and looks aft. The chain for the port side anchor can be seen at right. The fos'cle is often used for ceremonies, and on the morning when this photograph was taken, it was being prepared for one of these occasions.

FANTAIL

FORRESTAL was built with an open fantail as shown here. This was a feature she shared with her sister ship SARATOGA. Little more than a flagstaff was located on the fantail at the hangar deck level. (National Archives)

Today, the appearance of the fantail is far different. An engine test stand protrudes at the hangar deck level, and above it is the azimuth dome for the SPN-41 automatic landing control radar. A vertical series of lights stretches from below the hangar deck level up to the flight deck, and is a visual approach aid for pilots when landing.

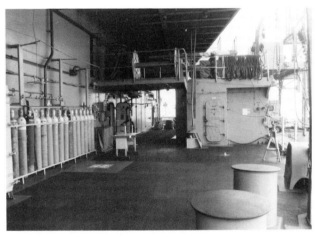

This view was taken from the port side of the fantail and looks to starboard.

This photograph was taken from the engine test stand area and looks to port.

A jet engine is being moved out onto the test stand area. Engines can be run up and tested on this stand for checkout and maintenance.

A boarding ladder is mounted on the fantail just to port of the centerline.

WEAPON SYSTEMS

Three Phalanx 20mm close-in weapon systems (CIWS) are installed on FORRESTAL to defend against anti-ship missiles and aircraft. This is the mount that is located on the port side forward.

Another system is mounted on the starboard side of the superstructure just below the auxiliary conning station. The weapon operates completely independent of the ship's other systems, and has proved very effective in a multiple threat environment and in the presence of countermeasures.

This is the mount on the superstructure during a firing exercise. The drone kills painted on the side of the mount attest to its accuracy.   (USS FORRESTAL)

The third Phalanx is located on the port quarter. This photograph shows that mount as seen from above and just forward of it. A canvas cover protects the barrels.

An early Mk 25 launcher for the basic point defense missile system (BPDMS), or Sea Sparrow missile was installed forward on the starboard side while FORRESTAL was being repaired in 1967-68 after her fire off Vietnam. A second similar launcher was installed on the port quarter in 1976. Here, the original launcher is shown firing a missile during practice exercises. (USS FORRESTAL)

Newer and more compact Mk 29 launchers have replaced the older variants. This is the starboard launcher as it appears today.

The port launcher is shown in this view that looks aft from the catwalk on the flight deck. The launcher can be seen beyond one of its two associated radars which is sponsoned out on its own small platform. The second radar is just above and to the left of the lower radar in this photo. As seen here, it is aimed almost straight up. The aft Phalanx gun system can be seen in the background.

This view looks down at the port launcher. One of its radars can be seen in the background.

This photograph shows the launcher on the port quarter firing a practice missile.

PROPELLERS & RUDDERS

FORRESTAL has four propellers, each with five blades. This photograph shows the two starboard propeller shafts and looks aft under the ship. The propeller has been removed from the outer shaft, while the propeller on the inner shaft is in place.

(U. S. Navy)

The photo above shows FORRESTAL's port rudder being replaced after servicing. Each rudder weighs forty-five tons. At right is one of the rudders after being removed from the ship following an extended cruise. After servicing, it will be replaced. *(Both U. S. Navy)*

BELOW DECKS

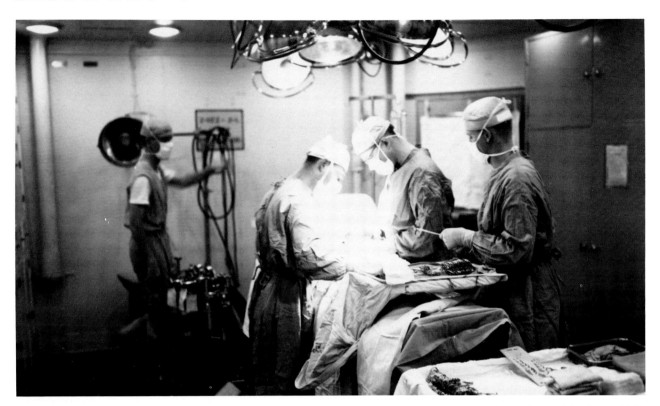

With the exception of hospital ships, aircraft carriers have the most complete medical facilities of any ships in the U. S. Navy. Fully equipped operating rooms are on each of the carriers. Often, sailors from other ships in the battle group are transferred to the carrier when their own ship's facilities cannot handle their medical needs. Here, an emergency appendectomy is being performed on a seaman from one of the other ships in FORRESTAL's battle group.

Above: This is a control console in the FORRESTAL's television studio. Several channels are available for the crewmen to watch, and programing ranges from movies to pre-recorded prime time television shows, to information channels. Live television shows can be made in the studio, but shows from the United States cannot be received and shown to the crew.

Right: Bunks for enlisted men are shown here. Crewmen store their clothing and other articles in small lockers and in these compartments in their bunk. The mattresses had been removed from the bunks when this photograph was taken. Bunks are arranged three high, and quarters are rather cramped. With well over 5000 men on board when the air group is embarked, it is impossible to provide much room for everyone, even on a ship the size of an aircraft carrier.

COMBAT DIRECTION CENTER & AIR OPS

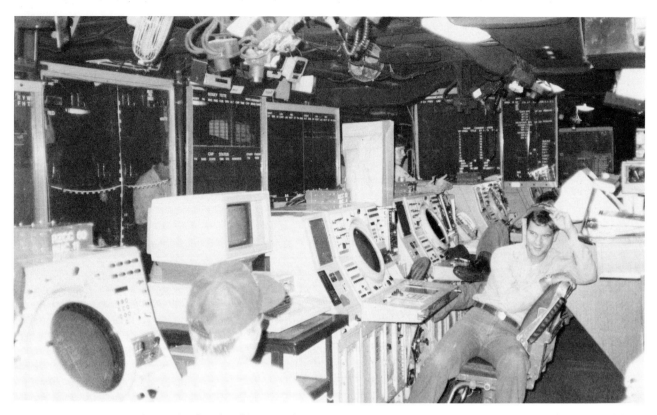

This photograph was taken in the Combat Direction Center while the ship was in port and not much was going on. When the ship is in action, CDC is a beehive of activity. Various consoles and boards keep operators appraised of the threat, weapon systems, and much more. While navigation of the ship is controlled from the bridge, it is here in CDC where FORRESTAL is controlled as a fighting ship.

These display boards are in Air Ops, and the status of all aircraft is maintained here. Anytime aircraft are outside the pattern, they are controlled from Air Ops. Once inside the pattern they come under the control of pri-fly.

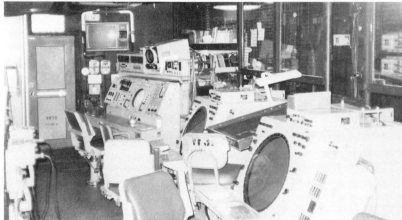

On the other side of the status boards are these consoles where aircraft are monitored and controlled.

DAMAGE CONTROL CENTRAL & ENGINE ROOM

Much of the ship is controlled from Damage Control Central, which is called DCC or simply Central. The ship's list is monitored here, and sea water is pumped between tanks to keep the carrier level as aircraft are moved around the decks. Much of the fire-fighting ability of the ship is controlled from here, as is the water that is used to supply steam to the catapults, the fire pumps, and fire mains. Any damage received in battle would also be controlled from DCC.

This is another view of DCC. In addition to the functions listed above, the ship's boilers are also controlled from here as are the alarm and electrical systems. In short, the men who work in DCC have many vital responsibilities and functions twenty-four hours a day.

These two photographs were taken in engine room number one. In the photograph at left, the number one main engine can be seen in the background, and at right is one of the boilers for this engine.

OFFICERS' MESS

This is the officers' formal dining area. The painting to the left in the photo is of FORRESTAL in her early configuration, and in the background is a portrait of James V. Forrestal, for whom the ship was named.

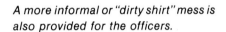A more informal or "dirty shirt" mess is also provided for the officers.

Just outside of the officers' dining area is a lounge with a television where off-duty officers can relax and visit.

ENLISTED MESS

These two photographs were taken in the chiefs' mess where the senior NCO's have their meals.

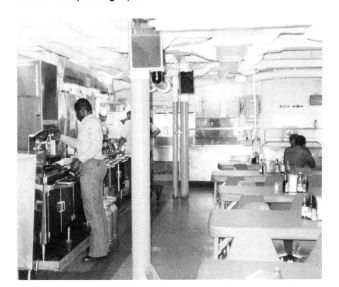

Most of the ship's crewmen eat in the enlisted mess, which is cafeteria style. While aboard, the author and photographer Donnie Head ate in both the officers' mess and the enlisted mess, and found the food to be quite good in both cases.

Over 22,000 meals are served daily when FORRESTAL is at sea with her air group. Keeping everyone fed is a full time job, and mess personnel prepare breakfast, lunch, and dinner, as well as snacks on an almost continuous basis. A good variety of food always seems to be available.

MODELERS SECTION

GENERAL COMMENTS

To date there have been five plastic kits released of the USS FORRESTAL. The oldest of these was a 1/542nd scale offering by Revell that first appeared in 1956, shortly after FORRESTAL entered service with the Navy. This kit was soon followed by a model from Aurora in 1/600th scale that fell far short of the Revell kit when it came to accuracy and quality. Although this Aurora kit was re-released by Monogram in the early 1980s, and included a new set of aircraft, it was not a kit that could be considered by serious modelers. This was because too many shapes were wrong, and would have been almost impossible to correct. The Monogram reissue still represented FORRESTAL in her original form, even though it was released over twenty years after the carrier had undergone extensive changes.

For many years, the original Revell and Aurora kits were the only ones that were available of FORRESTAL, but Revell got a lot of mileage out of their kit by re-releasing it as the other ships in the FORRESTAL class. Finally, in the 1987-88 time frame, Italeri produced a 1/720th scale model of FORRESTAL that was supposed to represent the ship as she now appears. It has been released in the United States by the Testors Corporation. Meanwhile, Revell took the molds for its original kit and made many of the updates necessary to make the model represent the carrier in her present form. In late 1989, Revell released its reworked kit as both FORRESTAL and SARATOGA.

The original Aurora kit was not around very long, and it is almost impossible to find one today, even at the largest of the collectors' swap meets. Because of this, and also because it was not a kit that could be considered by the serious modeler, we are not doing a full review of it or the subsequent reissue by Monogram in this modeler's section. We are using the space available by limiting our discussions to the Italeri/Testors release and the two Revell kits.

We hope that we have not seen the last kit of FORRESTAL to be released. Otaki/Arii has released some excellent carrier kits in 1/800th scale. While this is a very small scale, the number of aircraft carriers available in this scale is extensive, and an impressive collection can be built. Since KENNEDY has been released by Monogram and Minicraft, and since Otaki/Arii has released a large selection of carrier kits, of the U. S. Navy's currently active carriers, only the FORRESTAL class, LEXINGTON, and AMERICA are not available in this scale. (Arii's kit that claims to be AMERICA is actually a KITTY HAWK or CONSTELLATION.) With proper planning to allow for differences between the individual ships, one set of molds could be used as a basis to build all four ships in the FORRESTAL class, so at least four different releases could be done from the same molds. We sincerely hope that Arii or some other manufacturer will add a quality kit of a FORRESTAL class carrier to the already large selection of 1/800th scale aircraft carrier kits.

1/720th SCALE KIT

Italeri/Testors USS FORRESTAL, Kit Number 898

This is actually the second different kit of an aircraft carrier released by Italeri/Testors in this scale. The first was a NIMITZ class carrier that has been re-released a number of times as various ships of the NIMITZ class. It has also been marketed as the fictional GEORGETOWN from the short-lived television series "Supercarrier." In this release it was given the USS JOHN F. KENNEDY's number 67, but the model does not represent that ship at all. With all of the ship models that have been released in 1/700th scale, to include the excellent kits now being released by Skywave, as well as those by Hasegawa, Tamiya, and others, it seems strange that Italeri would choose 1/720th scale for its carrier models rather than 1/700th scale. Their models do not fit in collections with these other ships. The only previously released aircraft carrier in 1/720th scale was Revell's USS ENTERPRISE, and it is still the best carrier model in either 1/720th or 1/700th scale that is available today. Although Revell did release a few other ships in 1/720th scale, it seems that it would have been a much better decision for Italeri to stick with the much more popular 1/700th scale.

There is no way to build an accurate scale model of FORRESTAL from the Italeri/Testors kit without extensive reworking to make corrections. Additionally, many obvious features are missing and must be added by the modeler. Almost anywhere you look, there are serious inaccuracies. Considering the fact that this was a kit designed to represent the present day FORRESTAL from the beginning, rather than being a reworked kit, these inaccuracies are inexcusable.

The Testors kit is in 1/720th scale, and leaves a lot to be desired. Many hours will have to be spent by the modeler correcting errors and making additions if an accurate model is to be built from this kit.

On the port side of the superstructure is a bulge or blister. We have no idea what this is supposed to represent, but it certainly is not on the actual ship. Therefore, the port side of the island must be cut away and rebuilt from scratch by the modeler. Plastic card stock will do the job nicely. On the starboard side of the superstructure, the louvers are far too deep. They should be removed and rescribed to more accurately represent the real thing. Also on the island, the SEATEL dome is not the correct shape. It must be removed, and a new one that has been made from scratch should be put in its place. Many antennas are missing from the superstructure, the most noticeable of which are the two whip antennas that angle forward from the front of the island above the bridges. The radars that control the starboard Sea Sparrow launcher and missiles are also missing. The SPS-49 radar is inaccurate, and looks more like an SPS-43, which may be what Italeri was trying to represent. Our last comment about the superstructure is about the auxiliary conning station which is the wrong size and shape.

Moving down from the superstructure to the flight deck, we find more serious problems. The catapults are represented by oversized trenches, and are not lined up quite right. The most glaring and unforgivable problem here is that the trench for the number three catapult extends onto the number two elevator. It is hard to imagine how anyone developing a model could believe that part of a catapult could extend across a moveable elevator. All elevators are molded as part of the flight deck, and we would have preferred to see them separate so that the modeler could position them to his own taste without having to do plastic surgery. The supporting members beneath the elevators are very inaccurate and should be rebuilt. The JBDs behind cats one and two are not the correct size (they are not even the same size, and they should be), and they do not line up right. If you look at the photograph on the front cover, you will see that the outer edge of the JBD behind cat one is **inside** of the number one elevator. This is not the case with the model. Additionally, the catapult overruns are tapered rather than being rectangular like they should be.

If you compare the catwalks around the flight deck with those seen in the overhead views on the two covers of this book, you will see that the catwalks on the model are inaccurate. They are so bad that the only thing that can be done to correct them is to remove them and build new ones from scratch using thin plastic card. There is no detailing in these catwalks to speak of, and even the Belknap pole mast is missing. The arresting gear is also inaccurate, so we recommend filling the trenches for the catapults and those around the elevators with filler, then sanding the entire flight deck smooth. Then start over by adding the details accurately yourself. Lightly scribe the catapults to represent what is shown in this book, and scribe in JBDs that are correctly sized and located. Some modelers may want to use thin plastic card and show one or more of the JBDs in the raised position. As for the arresting gear, add small round fair lead sheaves and use thin stretched sprue to form the cross deck pendants.

Although the widened area of the flight deck is provided, it does not extend forward onto the number two elevator as it should. This must be added with plastic card. Representations of the fresnel lens, the elevation dome for the SPN-41 radar, and the LSO platform are all provided on the port side, but most modelers will want to rework them into more accurate and detailed replicas. Whip antennas that are located around the catwalks

should be made from thin stretched sprue.

The weapon systems pose more problems. Two poor representations of Sea Sparrow launchers are provided, but the problems don't stop there. A swallow's nest for the launcher on the starboard side forward is included in the kit, but the instructions tell you to place the launcher on the starboard quarter aft of the crane. FORRESTAL has no launcher in that location. The instructions show no launcher being positioned on the swallow's nest as there should be. There is no locating hole in either place. The other launcher goes on the port quarter, but again there is no locating hole, and no guidance radars to go with it. Italeri put the sponson for the forward Phalanx gun system on the port side in the proper location, but it is far too small. What is worse, no Phalanx gun is provided to go on it. In fact, there are no Phalanx systems in the kit, and no sponson for the one that goes on the port quarter. There is also no platform for the one that mounts on the starboard side of the superstructure. To solve these problems, we recommend using Sea Sparrow launchers and Phalanx CIWS from the Skywave kit SW-400, which provides parts for modern ships. Here, the scale problem comes into play again, since these parts are actually 1/700th scale. However, with a little work they can be made to look right. In any event, the modeler will have to replace the Phalanx sponson on the port bow, and build from scratch the sponson on the port quarter and the platform on the superstructure.

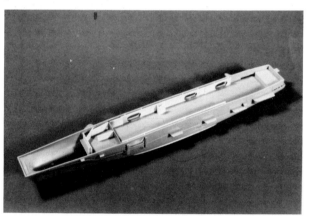

Adding a hangar deck to both the Revell and the Testors models will add a lot to the model. It will take a little time and effort, but will be well worth it. It is even better if the hangar deck is lighted with small light bulbs available from electronics stores and some railroad hobby shops. This is a Testors kit as seen while the hangar deck was being added. Double-walled sides to the hangar bays must also be added if the oval shaped openings for the elevators are to look right.

The hull also has its problems. The anchors are fair, but would look better if replaced by those from a photoetched sheet. The openings to the hangar bays are oval shaped, but are not the correct double oval openings they should be. Instead, each of the oval openings just extends back into an empty hull. These should be removed and proper openings made from plastic card. A hangar deck would be simple to make from plastic stock, and would add a lot to the model. The quarterdeck is inaccurate and incomplete, and the ship's crane mounted on the starboard quarter is incorrect. The boom portion of the crane needs to be rebuilt. The forward boarding deck on the port side is not enclosed as it should be.

Nowhere are there any railings molded in plastic. This is probably all right, since any modeler serious enough and good enough to turn this into an accurate model would probably want to add photoetched railings anyway. We recommend using Gold Metal Models sheet 720-11, which was designed for the Revell ENTERPRISE and the Testors NIMITZ kits. Railings, radars, and other detailed parts from this photoetched sheet can be used on this model, but hopefully Gold Metal Models, or some other company, will make a photoetched sheet designed especially for this model.

The model comes with a pitiful air group, which seems to be a problem with most carrier models. There are only six F-14s, three F-4s, three A-7s, three A-6s, two E-2s, and two SH-3 helicopters. The F-14s and F-4s should not be used together, so this reduces the size of the air group down to only sixteen aircraft if the F-14s are used, and thirteen aircraft if the F-4s are used. No S-3As or EA-6Bs are provided in this or any other carrier kit this scale. A 1/700th scale S-3A comes in DML kit number 7001 of the USS DALLAS and Typhoon submarines, and is also in the Testors reissue of this kit which is numbered 901. Although it is 1/700th scale, it does not look incorrect on this model. But there simply are not enough aircraft, nor enough types.

The decals are as poor as the rest of the kit. The 59 for the forward flight deck is way too large and is solid. FORRESTAL has used a small outlined 59 on her flight deck since her early years. There is only one 59 for the island, and it is not shadowed. There is a number on **both** sides of the real superstructure. The red and white dashed line (intended to be the foul line for the landing area) is too wide and the dashes are too long. The center stripe for the landing area is white and orange rather than the correct white and yellow. The elevator markings are far from complete, those for the armament elevators are too large, and the landing spots for the helicopters are incorrect. By using Gold Metal Models decal sheet 700-1D for 1/700th scale ships, some of these problems can be solved, but the landing lines should be painted on. The modeler is also faced with the problem of painting on the outlined 59 on the flight deck and coming up with a shadowed 59 for the starboard side of the superstructure.

All in all, this is a poor kit. On the positive side, it can be built as a full hull or waterline model, and this is a nice feature. The propellers look nice, and have wide blades. Many ship models have terrible propellers that look more like they belong on airplanes than ships. The kit also provides the barrel-shaped life rafts that go along the catwalks, and this is nice. But there are far more minuses than pluses for this kit. If one assumes that Italeri might

have been trying to model FORRESTAL before her SLEP conversion, some of the inaccuracies may be explained to some degree, but many more remained unexplained. We recommend that any modeler who wants to build an accurate model from this kit take his time and study the photographs in this book. Take each section of the ship, one at a time. Study the detailed photographs of it, then correct the model to look like the real thing. It will be a long and tedious process, but it will be the only way an accurate model can be built from this kit. We encourage Italeri and other kit manufacturers to release more ship models in 1/700th (not 1/720th) scale. If they do, we hope they will be more careful in their research before they begin to cut metal.

1/542nd SCALE KITS

Revell USS FORRESTAL, Kit Number H-339

When this kit was issued in 1956 at a retail price of $2.98, it was arguably the best plastic ship model ever released. It was quite detailed for its day, and fairly accurately represented the FORRESTAL as built. Revell went on to issue the kit as all carriers in the FORRESTAL class, making only minor changes. An enclosed fantail was provided for RANGER and INDEPENDENCE, and there were other minor differences. But some variations, such as those involving the lattice and main masts and the radar fits, were overlooked. More importantly, the differences in the forward gun sponsons between the ships were ignored.

This is the box art for the Revell FORRESTAL kit as it was first released in 1956.

The kit represented the ship in her "as built" configuration. All eight five-inch guns were included, the smoke stack was the original slanted version, and the aft mast represented the first one fitted to the actual ship. The two lattice masts on the starboard side hinged up and down, and the four elevators could be moved up and down on their guides. Detailing was excellent, and even included tiny representations of stairs, hoses, and reels in the catwalks. As originally issued, the six arresting cables and two barricades were molded into the flight deck. Both barricades were rigged, but were in the down or lowered position. All later reissues had the rigged barricades removed.

Not everything was completely accurate, and some

corrections had to be made. The bow dome was incorrect, not having a dome shape at all. This was because Revell wanted the hull to be molded in one piece, so mold release considerations meant that the dome could not be accurately represented. At the stern end, the propeller blades were far too thin, and the braces for the propeller shafts were incorrect. They were single pieces that extended from the shaft to the hull, but the real ones were V-shaped. The problems with the bow dome, the propellers, and the braces for the shafts could be eliminated by cutting the hull at the waterline and building a waterline model. One other problem below the waterline was the fact that the stabilizers on either side were missing. Building a waterline model would again solve this oversight, but they could easily be added if desired by the modeler. In fact, all problems below the waterline could rather easily be solved with the exception of scratch-building some accurate propellers.

Other problems with the kit included the fact that the forward Mk 56 gun directors were molded as part of the catwalks rather than being located under them, bumps were located around each of the elevators, and the openings to the hangar bays were deep ovals. As with any other carrier kit, adding a hangar deck would be a considerable improvement. Before doing so, cut away the inner portions of the ovals flush with the insides of the hangar deck walls, then add the inner walls and oval openings. Finally, add the hangar deck itself. Detailing can be added to the masts, guns, ship's crane, and the catwalks. Radars and railings are as good as they can be as represented by styrene plastic, but photoetched parts would be a big improvement. Hopefully one will be released soon for this kit and its updated cousin.

The air group was too small as usual, but what was provided was nicely done. Banshees, Furies, Cutlasses, Skywarriors, and two HUP helicopters were included. A few sink holes needed to be filled before the aircraft models could be added to the flight deck. Tractors and a tilly were also provided.

The decal sheet was excellent for its day, and was the first we know of to even include markings for the aircraft. The flight deck markings were the original ones with the three converging yellow lines and the yellow 59s at each end of the deck. Elevator markings were quite complete, and numerous other markings for the flight deck were included. Depth markings for the bow and stern were also on the decal sheet. About the only markings missing were those for the JBDs. Since all three JBDs were shown in the raised position, these markings would have been difficult to represent.

Since Revell has retooled the molds for this kit, there will be no more reissues of it in this form. But they are usually fairly easy to find on collector's tables, and we encourage any modeler that has one or can get one to take his time and build an outstanding model from it. The result will be well worth the effort.

Revell Updated USS FORRESTAL, Kit Number 5022

When we heard this kit was coming we were very excited. The original Revell kit was so outstanding for its day, and still held up pretty well more than thirty years after its release. But when we finally got our hands on one of these reworked kits, we were quite disappointed at first. What Revell did was to take its original kit and update it to represent FORRESTAL as she appears today. We were upset to see that so many of the updates had been done incorrectly or not at all. After studying the kit for some time and discussing it with representatives from Revell, we began to see that what was done to the kit was all that was possible within practical limits. The amount of money allocated to this project was considerable, and was still exceeded by a significant amount. Reworking an existing kit is not the same as doing a kit from square one. Since the expense required to start over from scratch was out of the question, no large model of FORRESTAL as she appears today would now be available had Revell not reworked its old model. In spite of the fact that much remains to be done, we are happy that Revell has taken the process this far, and a good modeler can take the kit the rest of the way. What needs to be done by the modeler is not difficult, but will take a considerable amount of time.

The reworked Revell kit comes in this box, and was released in 1989, over thirty years after the original release.

First we will summarize which updates Revell did make. The Sea Sparrow launchers are provided as are all three Phalanx weapon systems. The radars for the Sea Sparrow launcher on the port quarter are included, but the ones on the superstructure for the launcher on the starboard side are missing. The JBDs have been changed, but are still not correct. The simple thing to do is to leave them off, and use decals and scribing to represent their locations on the deck, thus showing them in their lowered positions. But building raised ones from plastic card would be a simple task. The fantail has also been updated, and it looks pretty good. However, many modelers will want to add more detailing, particularly around the engine test stand area. The approach lights and the azimuth dome for the SPN-41 radar are missing. The SPS-49 radar has been added to the superstructure, but it is not very good. Molding such intricate details as radars in plastic is most difficult, and here again we encourage someone to do a set of photoetched parts for this model.

Revell also added the life rafts that go around the flight

deck, but these leave something to be desired, and could be improved. We expect that budget constraints and the problem of working with the existing catwalks from the original kit caused Revell to have to do these rafts the way they did. The serious modeler will probably want to add rafts made from scratch. The mast and yardarm has been redone, but here again the modeler will need to rework them to get them to look right.

A completely new air group is provided with this kit, but again we would have liked to see more aircraft and a wider variety. The ones that are included are nice, but there are no A-7 Corsairs and no E-2 Hawkeyes. No other kit provides them in this scale. We would like to see Revell issue aircraft kits with the aircraft supplied in this kit as well as the missing E-2s and A-7s. Other manufacturers of carrier kits have done this, and it would eliminate the problem of not enough aircraft and not enough different types of aircraft. A-6Es, EA-6Bs, F-14s, S-3As and SH-3s are provided, and are nicely done.

There are a lot of things that were left off of this kit that the modeler will have to add. Perhaps the most noticeable of these is the flight deck extension just aft of the number two elevator. The designers at Revell told us there was simply no way to modify the molds to add this to the existing deck or to change the deck so that it would accept a new and separate piece. So the modeler must get some plastic stock and add this extension himself. Keep in mind that a small part of this extension goes forward on to the number two elevator. The forward boarding or boat deck on the port side was not enclosed, but remains in its original open configuration, so this must be modified with some plastic card stock. The Mk 56 gun directors that were molded into the original forward catwalks still remain, and these must be removed. The saluting guns are not present on the port side, so the catwalk needs to be altered to accept them, then the guns should be added. The quarterdeck will also need some work.

The flight deck still has six arresting cables and two barricades, so these must be updated. FORRESTAL now only has four cables and one barricade. Only the sup-

ports for the barricades are etched into the deck, so the forward pair are easily removed. The light units at each corner of the flight deck are still provided as separate pieces, and these should not be used. They were removed from FORRESTAL during her early operational life. The two lattice masts also remain in the kit, and they have long since been removed from the real ship.

All of the problems below the waterline that we discussed in our review of the original kit still remain with this release, and we will not repeat them again here. But check our comments about these inaccuracies in the review above before you build this model. Again, the easy way to get around them is to build a waterline model. The same could be said about the deep oval openings to the hangar bays. These remain the same as before, and should be corrected as explained in our review of the original kit. Then add a hangar deck so that the model does not have a hollow look.

Many small improvements and additions will also have to be made. The canisters on the base of the former gun sponson on the starboard quarter should be removed and replaced with cylinders made from sprue. The auxiliary conning station on the superstructure should be updated, and the bumps around the elevators need to be removed. An elevation dome for the SPN-41 radar, a fresnel lens, and the LSO's platform need to be added or improved as appropriate. Smaller antennas, such as the two large whip antennas that angle forward from the superstructure must be added, and whip antennas around the flight deck need to be replaced with thinner ones. Supporting members under the elevators will have to be built from scratch. There is much more that needs to be done, and much more that can be done.

The decals are quite nice except for the foul lines and those that are supposed to go around the armament elevators and the cover for the rigging for the barricade. Paint on the foul lines, and scrounge some red and yellow dashed lines (like those around the aircraft elevators) to use around the armament elevators and cover for the barricade rigging. Don't use the decals for the barricade supports, and although they are satisfactory, we recommend not using the decals for the landing lines. Paint these lines on instead.

Again, we suggest that the modeler take each section of the carrier step by step. Study the photographs of each section in this book, then build, modify, and correct that part of the model to look like the real thing. With a lot of time and patient work, an excellent model can result. Carrier models in this scale are far more impressive than the smaller 1/700th, 1/720th, and 1/800th scale models.

This is the new Revell model as displayed by the manufacturer at the RCTA hobby show at Chicago in October of 1989. Many updates were made to the kit, but the modeler still has a lot of work to do if an accurate model is to be built of FORRESTAL as she appears today.